W9-BUP-857

Encounters on the Way

Nourished by Life

ROBERT J. SUDERMAN

Encounters on the Way
Copyright © 2020 by Robert J. Suderman

All rights reserved. No part of this publication may be
reproduced, distributed, or transmitted in any form or by
any means, including photocopying, recording, or other
electronic or mechanical methods, without the prior
written permission of the author, except in the case of
brief quotations embodied in critical reviews and certain
other non-commercial uses permitted by copyright law.

tellwell

Tellwell Talent
www.tellwell.ca

ISBN
978-0-2288-3351-2 (Paperback)

Dedication

These reflections are dedicated to my various circles of family. I am grateful to you all.

The first circle is my wife Irene, our children and grandchildren. Some have been encouraging me to write something of this nature for a very long time. Irene is captain of those. Thank you for your persistence and encouragement — even when you thought it was a lost cause. I am grateful to you and love you very much. The children: Bryan and Julie; Derek and Rebecca; Andrew and Karen (in order of appearance): Thank you for making ours a very good family. And thank you for your thoughtfulness with us and care for us. And our grandchildren: Matthew, Zoe, Eden, Samantha, James, and Simon (in order of appearance). Thank you for being you with us. I hope that this window into the life of your grandfather will be helpful to you at some point in your lives. Maybe it can explain some of your own idiosyncrasies or help you understand the peculiarities of your parents — or at least your fathers. We love you very much — each one.

There is the circle of my childhood family: my seven siblings, their spouses, and nieces and nephews. You have shaped me more than you know. I am fortunate to have grown up with you. I thank each of you for your part in that. My father and mother — and later my stepmother — are, obviously, key pillars in what I have written and in what I have become. Each one of them left too early. I'm sad about that. But they have never been forgotten, and I am grateful for their unyielding support.

There is the circle of Irene's family. When we marry, we enter another family system that begins to influence who we are. Thank you — to each one — for accepting me into your family as you have. You have made our life richer and better. Your parents (my in-laws) have been supportive to our endeavours. We miss them very much. I am grateful for each one.

And then there is the whole host of extended family. There were seventy-seven first cousins just on my father's side. I don't know how many there were on my mother's side. I was too young to get to know them before they moved west. One cannot grow up in such a large circle of family without being impacted by them. I am proud to say that the impact from you has been positive. Thank you; I am grateful.

I am grateful to God who has walked with us so far. And I trust that the pieces of life that remain to be written will also be lived to the fullest.

Foreword

In this short book I have attempted to highlight some of the elements that contributed to making me who I am. It is, of course, entirely insufficient. There are countless more episodes in my life that consciously or unconsciously have shaped both my experience and my memory of the experience — and these two may not be the same.

I write from the perspective of the youngest of eight siblings. There were fifteen years between the oldest brother and me. I am well aware that the experience of the youngest may not at all be what the older ones experienced. Things changed. Times changed. But this is what I remember.

In writing this manuscript, I've become increasingly aware that memory is slippery. At times it feels like a wild animal, roaming free without fences. Other times it feels like a hamster in a cage, not quite getting access to what is desired in spite of frantically running on the exercise wheel. Supposedly, memory helps us acquire information, organize and file it away, and then recall it accurately. But it's clear that somewhere in that process other things creep in. What I recall is not necessarily exactly what happened — even though I'm convinced it is. A few times, I was able to check the historical evidence of what I remember, and I discovered my memory was wrong. I can only imagine how often that is also true of the experiences that I have not been able to check out. And so, I offer a humble disclaimer to my siblings, other readers, and to future historians alike who might wish to use these encounters as precise evidence of how it really was: Please allow for potential discrepancies.

It has, however, been fun to remember. I trust that these encounters may be interesting to others, and perhaps even helpful in some way.

Robert J. Suderman
July, 2020

Table of Contents

Dear Reborn:

Thanks so much for being part of the
fertilizer, Sun and rain of my Life.
And thanks for your warm and caring
friendship over so many years,
With deep appreciation and Love,
Jack

December 25, 2020

Collage of home-farm buildings
Beginning on the left: house, granary, chicken barn, animal
barn. Missing are the pig sty and the workshop

I

Early Life

An Overview

My birth name is Robert John, but apparently from day one my parents called me Jackie. Why? I don't know. I have never heard a clear explanation. But Jackie it was. As I grew and matured a bit my name changed to Jack, although my sister continues to call me Jackie whenever she can. As far as I remember, I was never called Robert or John. Robert became the preferred name when we moved to Latin America in 1980. Jack does not really work in Spanish. Roberto works perfectly. So legally, and in Latin America, Asia, Africa, and Europe I am Robert J. In North America, I am Jack. Go figure. Either one is fine.

I grew up on a subsistence farm in southern Manitoba — in the Greenfarm School District, to be exact. Our school district was 6 kms. from the small town of Winkler, now a significant city. We were 25 kms. from the USA border, and 150 kms. from Winnipeg.

My parents owned 180 acres of farmland — very little compared to most of our neighbours. We had some cattle for milk and cream; pigs for slaughter and cash; chickens for meat and eggs; and we had Birdie: a larger than life, beautiful horse that became my daily companion when I got a bit older. Riding Birdie bareback across the vast fields was heaven. She was fast and warm. We would chase foxes and rabbits. I could ride her all winter.

We had a large garden that produced food for the winter, much of it canned, of course. We had an old red Farmall H tractor, and an even older, green Oliver tractor. The farm machinery was second-hand — a small combine, swather, plow, cultivator, and harrow. Often, during the height of the growing season, my father would spend his time fixing the machinery when it should be on the field being productive.

I was the youngest of eight children: five boys and three girls. We had a small house. Two bedrooms upstairs and one downstairs for my parents. The boys slept together in one bedroom, the girls in the other. We had a coal-burning, pot-bellied stove that worked valiantly to keep the poorly insulated house warm enough in -40C degree weather. The stove pipes that wound their way up through the ceiling and the upstairs would sometimes get red-hot. How the house never burned down, given the wood-chip insulation, is beyond lucky.

My parents were devout Christians. My dad, a cautious man, was the only one with a Grade 11 education in his family of eleven siblings. He tried teaching for a year or two, but ended up on the farm — close to his parents and brothers. His sisters married and moved elsewhere. My mother was a strong-willed woman. She preferred reading and writing to cooking and baking. She wrote a weekly article for the *Winkler Progress* detailing all the comings and goings of the twenty or so Greenfarm School District families. She had a chronic heart condition, and was often sick, resting, and in bed. My dad did most of the baking; my sisters did the cooking and cleaning.

Wedding photo of my parents: Jacob Suderman
and Margaret Epp, June 28, 1928.

I went to a country school: Greenfarm. It began as a one-room school. In kindergarten, I was one of fifty-two students with one teacher in one class ranging from K-10. I had six siblings in that same classroom. The rest were mostly cousins. The district was made up — mostly — of four extended family units: Sudermans, Driedgers, Ennses, and Hildebrands. These were offspring of the courageous folks that migrated from Russia to Manitoba in the 1870s. After kindergarten, the district added one more room to the school, with Grades 1-4 in one room, and 5-8 in the other. The idea was that for Grades 9-12, we would attend the high school in Winkler.

I was a farm boy. I was milking cows, feeding chickens and pigs, and gathering eggs at the age of seven. In the winter, I helped take the manure out of the barn with the horse and sled. We were 3 kms. from the school. Much of the time I would walk; in winter, Dad would take us by horse and sled; in fall and spring, I also used the bicycle. My childhood was happy. Friends, family, church, school, and chores: there was purpose and meaning every day. If I got lazy or didn't do what was expected, the cows would moo to be milked, the chickens would cackle to be fed, the pigs would whine. These were daily reminders that what I was assigned to do was important. It mattered.

Jack as a young lad

I did well in school, always competing for top spot in my grade (of five students) with a girl who was my neighbour. My parents had a rule that each child had to sit out school for one year to learn other things important for life. My turn was in Grade 9, but my mother thought it would be a good idea to take that year by correspondence. And so I did. I did very little work. My mom helped me pass the bi-weekly tests, and I passed with a 51% average. I quickly recovered, however, after enrolling — on probation — in Gr. 10 in the Winkler High School.

Hours spent honing skills at pitching.

Our church building was in Winkler: The Winkler Bergthaler Church. We went every Sunday morning — without fail. My father was one of three *Vorsaenger,* choosing the right hymns for the service. By and large we did not go to Sunday School: that was for the town kids. Later I did sing in the choir and attended youth events. The services were in High German, with a mini and a maxi sermon every Sunday. The mini one was called the *Einleitung* (Introduction), and was usually given by one of the deacons. The maxi was given by one of the ministers. When Deacon Loewen prayed, we would time the length. He was capable of having 10-15 minute prayers. He was sincere. We were bored. Singing was hearty and always four-part harmony. When we got home, more often than not, there was a family or two of uncles, aunts, and cousins waiting for us. My mother would add more potatoes to boil, and a few more slabs of pork to the menu. Sometimes families with thirteen children would arrive — unannounced — for Sunday lunch.

At some point on Sunday afternoon, we would go see Grandma and Grandpa, who lived several miles away. Many uncles, aunts, and cousins would drop in for *faspa* (late afternoon lunch). It was not unusual for there to be thirty to fifty people there, including children, of course. These were great times with some assortment of my seventy-seven cousins. Adult supervision was not needed nor welcome. The ball diamond in summer and the hayloft in winter were all we needed to keep entertained.

Looking back now, I realize what a good and healthy childhood I had, in spite of the hard times my parents must have experienced.

Suderman tribe: 1939; Grandparents Abram Suderman (1871-1958) and Margaretha Driedger (1874-1954) in the middle; my mother second from right 2nd row; my father second from right 3rd row. The oldest 4 of 8 siblings are in the picture, along with 41 of 77 first cousins.

Worship Wars as a Seven-Year-Old

My father was a *Vorsaenger* in church. I believe he did that for over forty years. When he decided to quit, the church elders eliminated the position in favour of more modern ways. There were three *Vorsaenger*: Suderman, Friesen, and Siemens, and two hymnals: the *Gesang Buch* and the *Evangeliums Lieder*. The *Gesang Buch* had more sombre, slow-moving songs. The *Evangeliums Lieder* was more upbeat, with Fanny Crosby and such. These three men would sit on the platform next to the pulpit. They did not know the theme of the day (if, indeed, there was one). They did not know the title of the sermon (if, indeed, there was one). Their job was four-fold: to know their hymnals well; to listen to the tone and messages of the deacons and ministers; to choose appropriate hymns that would speak to the mood and the messages provided; and to lead out in singing — after getting a pitch from a trusty tuning fork that was always handy in their pockets.

Looking back, I realize that this process was, perhaps, the closest we ever got to Pentecostal-style leading of the Spirit. The more or less formal ritual was that about half-way through the sermon, the *Vorsaenger* whose turn it was to choose the after-sermon song, would pick up one of the hymnals and soberly begin to scan the pages, all the while listening carefully to the sermon. When the sermon ended, the *Vorsaenger* would, spontaneously, be prepared to announce the song. The process was designed to be "Spirit-led." The Spirit would provide insight into the most appropriate song to sing after hearing the stirring message. As children, we would watch carefully. If we saw the *Vorsaenger* choosing the *Gesang Buch*, we would groan. When we saw him reach for the *Evangeliums Lieder* we began to rejoice. We liked those lively songs more. Usually Suderman and Friesen were fairly balanced in their choice of hymnals. Siemens was a *Gesang Buch* fan. Given that there were usually four hymns sung during a service, we became expert in anticipating the choice of the song book.

I learned very early, perhaps beginning at age seven, that my father was in a hazardous vocation. He was in a no-win situation. Most in the congregation, it seemed, were aligned with one hymnal or the other. He would attract criticism no matter which hymnal he chose. I would observe what appeared to be heated conversations with my dad after most services. When we finally managed to get home, usually just after we sat down for dinner, the party-line phone would begin to signal our number. My father would patiently get up from dinner and answer the phone, knowing that a goodly number of neighbours were listening in to the party-line call. Some well-meaning but critical soul would call and complain about the hymn he had chosen. My dad would listen, explain that he was choosing hymns based on the content of the message, not based on the hymn book, and asked for understanding. This routine happened not at all infrequently. Sunday meals were often interrupted at least once by a less than happy church attender.

I realize now that the "worship wars" we speak of today are not at all new. My father navigated over forty years of such struggles. It led him to understand his role as a critically important one in the life of the congregation. What he did mattered to many. And it mattered very much to him. I suspect I learned more than I know by becoming ever more aware of the dynamics he faced. His gentle, accommodating, patient spirit was a lesson for us all.

Excitement and Compassion on December 23

We lived on a small farm. The family economy was not strong — it was tentative and vulnerable. In Manitoba, rain is the annual referee, determining if the crops would be good, normal, or bad. There were no guarantees. I remember the happiest days of my childhood were when the rains came. A three-day rain would, more or less, guarantee a good year. Then we would stay inside, play games, and my parents were happy. I think it was their evident hopeful attitude that embedded hope in my heart when it rained. It still happens today.

In 1956 when I was 11 years old, all seemed to go well. Crops were good and promising. Then one very hot July day we saw the threatening clouds in the west. Slowly they built and surrounded our farm with lightning and thunder. But this time it was not rain. It was a heavy hail storm. Ice pellets, some the size of golf balls, pelted down. We took shelter where we could. I don't know how long it lasted, but it was too long.

When it was over, my father and older brothers went out to assess the damage. The news was bad — very bad. With time, it became apparent that our farm, and only our farm, was totally devastated. It was almost as if God had targeted us. No one else in Greenfarm was hailed out. We would not have a crop or garden that year. I was too young to know exactly what this all meant for my parents, but the mood in the home indicated it would be a tough year.

Our country school Christmas program was always slated for December 23. The teachers and students rehearsed for months to get ready for it. We were convinced each year was the best program ever. It was a community event: everyone was there. And we, nervously, played our parts in the little dramas, we sang our songs, recited our poems, and we heard the Christmas story. Then — the highlight — we received little brown paper bags from the school board. These bags were fill with peanuts, some candy, and a mandarin orange. It was all very exciting.

That year, the December 23 program progressed as usual on a cold and wintry night. When we went back to the car to drive home, a surprise awaited us. We saw that the car was full of harvest products: carrots, potatoes, peas, onions, even beef and pork. My parents were overwhelmed. There was again a spark of hope in our home. The community had organized to help our family through the rough, hailed-out year. There was a sincere sense of joy and gratitude that filled the house when we got home. Not only would Christmas be good, the produce would last until the next garden would yield its fruit.

As I look back, I am again convinced that I learned more than I realized. The importance and strength of community was surely deeply embedded in my being. To this day I am glad I experienced first-hand how that can look and what that can mean.

The Coming of the Evangelists

The 1950s were interesting years. There was change in the air, but no one was quite sure if it was good or bad. A little later, Elvis Presley sang a heart-rending rendition of *How Great Thou Art*. It was the same Elvis who was leading the youth astray with his swaying hips, long sideburns, and rock music. This same person could convincingly sing *How Great Thou Art*? I remember my parents' struggle with how to understand this.

But Elvis wasn't the only intruder into the serene lives of the farming and church communities around Winkler. Somewhere during that time, someone was convinced that Mennonites in southern Manitoba needed to be "saved." The fact that the huge majority of folks were in the church were baptized, lived upright lives, and were God-fearing, golden-hearted folks, was, apparently, not enough. We also needed to be saved.

I don't know exactly where this came from. Now, with the studies I've done, it seems that it was a wave that came through the US Christian community and was then rapidly assimilated in Canada. And so the evangelists began to come to Winkler. There was Brunk, Neufeld, and the Jantz brothers. They were invited into the community by the common assent of the inter-church ministerial committee — the first miracle. They came in summer. Large tents and loud-speakers were set up in the fairgrounds in Winkler, I believe. The local congregations were encouraged to promote the attendance of everyone. It was a special time — usually a week — for the never-yet-saved to take that step, and an opportunity for the backsliders — which included everybody — to get back on the right track. Sinners could become saints, and the saints could recognize and confess their repeated sins. The pressure was on: ministers were watching who was not attending.

I always had a sense that my parents were not particularly in favour of these events — especially my mother. It seemed as though they would go — and take us — out of obligation, not out of personal conviction. But we went. The music was fantastic. The mass choirs sang with gusto and conviction. The soloist cried every night as he sang *How Great Thou Art*. And then the sermon: it was dynamic, interesting, and very forthright. The sermon painted a picture of each one's personal sinfulness. And, it's true, there was enough sin to go around in our community. The sermon then painted a Technicolor picture of what happens when sin is not confessed. This usually included an early, unexpected death, and the potential of eternal, fiery damnation. It was dramatic. And then the sermon provided the recipe to deal with that sin and to be saved — once again, or for the first time. The solution was to receive Jesus into our hearts. Confidence abounded that this could be achieved by repeating a short prayer. But this needed to be done publicly. Otherwise, it wasn't necessarily real.

The signature event of the evening was to make a public confession of our conversion by "coming forward." Then all could see and our commitment was no longer internal, between God and me. It was a communal event. By coming forward, I could pronounce my personal intention to change my life, and the community could surround me with the love and tools I would need to make that conversion real. It was an intriguing synthesis of the more evangelical insistence on internal, vertical experience with the Spirit of God, and the "Mennonite" insistence on communal accountability, discipleship, and discipline.

The mechanism used for the invitation to come forward was the singing of *Just as I Am*, written by Charlotte Elliot in 1835:

> *Just as I am — without one plea, but that thy blood was shed for me,*

And that thou bidst me come to Thee, O Lamb of God,
I come; I come.

Designated deacons and others would roam the aisles, seeing if they could make eye contact with anyone who was wavering. If so, they would tap the shoulder and encourage the person — young or old — to come forward. If there wasn't enough response to coming forward, then the last verse would be repeated, and repeated again. I remember that song felt eternal, especially for those who, like me, resisted the invitation. This could be my last chance. I might be killed in a traffic accident tomorrow like the evangelist's friend was last week. I think it was my sense of my parents' reticence that kept me from going forward. I wasn't sure if they would have approved or not. So I didn't go, in spite of the significant pressure I felt to do so. And, of course, because I allowed such human considerations to stand in the way, I was all the more guilty of sin and blocking the work of the Spirit. It was a no-win situation.

I remember one time I went to the service with Dad; this time it was in our church, not in a tent. Mr. Neufeld, a giant of a man with a booming voice, was the invited evangelist. We went a bit early as we always did. We walked into the foyer of the church and there was Mr. Neufeld. He briefly welcomed us, shook my father's hand and in a loud voice asked him: "Are you saved?" My father, always a cautious person, was silent for a moment. He straightened up, looked up at Mr. Neufeld, and responded: "I think that's a question my neighbours would have to answer. Why don't you ask them?" It was clear to me, even as an eleven-year-old boy, that Mr. Neufeld was not pleased. Now I better understand: for Mr. Neufeld, my father's answer likely bordered on "works-righteousness" — one of the heresies the evangelists wanted to stamp out. But that's where the conversation ended.

I think I learned more than I realized from the evangelists and from this incident with my father. As gentle as always, my father had provided an alternative vision of what it means to be "saved." He didn't preach it, he just lived it. The impact of that lesson is with me to this day.

The Limitations of Formal Education: Lessons from My Mother

Apparently, my mother's heart was damaged giving birth to me — the last of eight children. She suffered with heart issues as long as I knew her. She died young, at the age of fifty-nine. She spent much time in bed or lying on the couch. She read a lot, and was always wading through one more *Reader's Digest* condensed book. She wrote a weekly news article for the *Winkler Progress* newspaper. Her job was to write about the Greenfarm news. It seemed to make her both the hero and the villain in Greenfarm. Sometimes she wrote about things that Greenfarmers didn't want others to know about.

She was the daughter of a Bergthaler church minister. Her parents and most of her sixteen siblings moved from Manitoba to BC and Alberta early in my mother's marriage. I didn't get to know her side of the family well. I don't remember ever meeting my grandparents on my mother's side.

Only recently have I discovered that my Grandmother Epp (my mother's mother) was a feisty, outspoken, and quite opinionated pastor's wife. Apparently, she would write letters of critique about various issues in the church. I now have a new perspective from which to understand my mother. She too was made of different stuff. When she met with her sisters-in-law, she was a bit of an outsider. She wanted to discuss the latest book she had read. They wanted to share recipes and talk about raising their children. I suspect that if they had lived in another era, both my mother and grandmother would have applauded and supported the women's liberation movements. They were both free thinkers.

I suspect it was my mother's idea that each of the children should spend at least one school year at home learning about life beyond arithmetic, reading, and writing. My turn came in Grade 9, which made sense. By that time, our country school only had Grades 1-8, and we were considered too young to go to the big town school already in Grade 9. My mother's solution was for me to stay home and take Grade 9 by correspondence. This meant enrolling with the Department of Education and receiving weekly assignments in all of the designated classes: English, history, mathematics, science, and so on. I needed to work at the assignments, do the readings, and then write tests based on the materials of the previous two weeks.

I relished staying at home. My older brother, already finished high school, was also at home. He was the only one of the children that seemed to have an aptitude to be a farmer and, perhaps, someday taking over the family farm. All the other siblings were either in school or already working to support our family income.

My schedule was full: playing crokinole, chess, and checkers with my brother and father; doing the chores; cleaning the barn. I spent much time outside practicing my baseball pitch with my brother, riding my bike, and going for rides on Birdie, our beautiful horse. In fall, I helped with the sugar beet harvest — an important new initiative that was finally providing some cash for my parents. There didn't seem to be much space in my schedule for schoolwork. My mother encouraged me to be as busy as possible. She always gave me a sense that I was learning important things in the activities I was involved in.

I didn't have a regular schoolwork schedule. This meant that when the two-week tests came along, I was far from ready. My mother was the designated adult trusted by the department to administer the tests. Most of the time, I was woefully unprepared because I simply had not done the assigned work. My mother was serenely disinterested in my success or failure. The important thing, she said, was to somehow pass the tests. When she noticed that I didn't have the skills or the data to respond to the test questions, she would regularly open a particular textbook to a designated page and point to where I could find the useful information. This was, of course, entirely prohibited by the department, but she was undeterred. She simply repeated that during this year I was learning other important life lessons. It was always a bit of a mystery to me — and still is — exactly what those life lessons were. But I took her word for it.

Needless to say, I did not do well on tests. My marks usually came back hovering around the 50% mark — a situation entirely unusual for me, as I had excelled in my grades in the previous years. My mother was not worried. I passed the year "on probation" with a 51% average. This meant that I could enrol in Grade 10 with the proviso of a first term probationary period. If I did not do well, I would be put back into Grade 9.

I enrolled in the Winkler High School for Grade 10 and was put into the "probationary" classroom. By Christmas time I was not only the head of my class, but closing in on the high scorers in the regular class. My mother was right: I didn't need to sit through each grade. There were other things to learn to prepare me for life. I have, however, noticed the educational gap in some ways. To this day, I am amazed when others my age know who the British kings and queens were. I didn't, and I don't. British history was one of the subjects I sort of passed in Grade 9.

But the lesson from my mother has remained with me. Much later, a teacher colleague of mine kept insisting that schools are made for students, not students for schools. It was a perspective that my mother would have signed on to. It has become part of my pedagogical mantra ever since.

My Encounter with Royalty: Princess (Queen) Elizabeth and I

It was Tuesday, October 16, 1951. I was six years old, and the hype in Canada had been building. Princess Elizabeth's visit to Winnipeg and other parts of Canada had been postponed due to King George VI's serious illness. But now the day was here. Her Royal Highness would be visiting Winnipeg. My parents decided that such an historical event should not pass us by. In spite of a chronic shortage of cash, we would miss school and go to see the princess. We had a 1941 Chevrolet. We prepared for the trip. Eight children and our parents piled into the car. My mother, father, and oldest brother and I were in the front seat. I was assigned to the lap of my oldest brother. The other six siblings were in the back seat.

A trip to the big city was a big deal. I believe it was my first time ever. Almost half-way there, we stopped at a gas station where there was also a bathroom and where ice cream cones were sold. It was good to get out and stretch. Much to our surprise, my oldest brother, who had already been out working for several years, offered to buy us all an ice cream cone. This was an unprecedented blessing.

We enjoyed our cones and climbed back into our pre-assigned seating arrangement. I climbed up on my brother's lap. While I was adjusting my comfort level, he closed the car door. The problem was that my fingers were still grabbing hold of the upper part of the door frame. One of my fingers was crushed in the door. I yanked my hand away, and by doing so I pulled out the fingernail from the bottom roots up. The pain was modest because the finger was numb. There was a scramble to see how serious it was. It was indeed serious. The question arose whether we needed to turn back to see a doctor. My father indicated that if I continued to cry, we would need to cancel the trip and go back. If not, we could proceed. There was no way that I wanted to miss the big trip — and miss meeting the princess. Neither did I want to be the one responsible for all the others missing their trip. So, I stifled my cries of the pain that was slowly building. My mother invented a bandage out of a handkerchief and tied it tightly around my finger. It seemed that I would be able to live with it. The trip continued.

We arrived in Winnipeg and found a place along the car route that the princess would be taking. We had a frontline view among the thousands who had come out to watch. The parade of cars began to approach very slowly. The crowds were cheering, and we could see the princess waving and smiling. As they approached our location, I waved vigorously with my hand with the tied up finger. The princess looked at me and waved back. I was elated. Our trip was a resounding success.

Later, of course, folks mocked my insistence that the princess had looked directly at me and waved just for me. It was just the excited imagination of a six-year-old, they said. It could be. But it's not the way I remember it.

After the cars were gone, the crowds began to disperse. We found our way to the Assiniboine Park, where we enjoyed a picnic lunch. And we were ready to head back home. What a marvellous day.

The next day, we went to the doctor. The roots of the fingernail had been torn out. He took it off and cut off the surrounding damage. To this day, I have the crucified leftovers of the fingernail on my left hand. But I did not cry all day, and we saw the princess — but more than that, she saw me. An unforgettable experience.

Youth Group Bowling and Selling Cars: Misdemeanours and Holy Living

My adolescent and youth years happened in the 1950s and early 1960s. These were turbulent years in society in general but especially in Mennonite communities. These years saw the birth of rock and roll and it's most popular agent, Elvis Presley. These were the years of the Beatles, long hair, mini-skirts, and contraceptive pills. They were years of the unpopular war in Vietnam and the women's liberation movements. Especially in the USA, they were the years of social and racial unrest, and the assassinations of Martin Luther King Jr., and Robert and John F. Kennedy. They were the years of free love and the social ridiculing of religion, especially the Christian faith. They were the years of protest and Bob Dylan. Inside our church, these were the years of shifting from German to English language in worship, and the shift from lay to professional pastoral leadership. Nothing, it seemed, was sacred anymore. Everything could and should be questioned. Old answers didn't hold water.

Mennonite leaders were overwhelmed with the fast-moving changes in public attitudes. This societal tsunami also impacted the attitudes and worldviews of Mennonite churchgoers. Of course, there were many traditions and values that were old but good. Values that should be maintained. But the social revolution upended the apple carts first, and then looked to see if there were still good apples later. It was, undoubtedly, a very complex time for leadership.

Our young generation began to question some of the traditional values of the church and its habits. To its credit, our church experimented by hiring a youth minister — the first ever. We liked Pastor Friesen. He had some interesting ideas. He had lived in Germany for many years and came with a broader orientation to life and church. He noted what was happening within our youth group. There was too much drinking, too much illicit dating, too many early pregnancies. There was little approved activity for young people in the church. There was the Friday night choir practice, the catechism church membership preparation classes, and in the winter there was Friday night skating at the local rink. Beyond that, most activities were not allowed as church activities.

Pastor Friesen was convinced we needed more supervised social time together. He proposed the idea of a bowling night in a neighbouring town. Such activity was generally considered too frivolous for church sponsorship. How can bowling bring us closer to the Lord? The church elders opposed his idea; the young people were excited about it. Pastor Friesen took us bowling — once. We had a great time. There were serious discussions happening behind closed doors. Pastor Friesen kept his job, but we never went bowling together again. I don't know what happened, but we had a taste of what could be. And we had tasted the potential power of youth.

The changing times, however, did not impact only the youth. I remember my father talking about some significant church conversations having to do with a car salesmen in our church. Winkler had Ford, Chevrolet, and Chrysler dealerships. One of the key values of the church was truth-telling, honesty, and transparency. How are these things related? One of the church members had changed his place of employment from a Chevrolet to a Ford dealership. For us now, that doesn't seem like a big deal. But then, it was an issue. He was a very good salesperson, was convinced about the superiority of Chevrolet over Ford, and he had a faithful following of people who had been convinced by him — all Chevrolet drivers. And now, he was going to sell cars at the Ford dealership and use his significant gifts of persuasion to sell Ford products. How can this happen? After years of developing his integrity as a Chevrolet man, how could he possibly, with integrity, now change horses and sell Ford products? Had he been lying all these years? Or was he lying now? I understood that there were even some suggesting that this car salesperson should be disciplined by the church because his word and his life actions didn't seem to align. Jesus taught us that our yes should be yes and our no should be no. And yet here he was changing his persuasive powers from Chevrolet to Ford. Had he broken with an essential ethical doctrine of the church? After all, the church taught that honesty, truth-telling, and integrity were the DNA of the church's teachings. Was he not flaunting this integrity by switching sides? I believe he stayed on as member, but it wasn't assumed that he could.

These two cases indicate how much stress and struggle church leadership was under. They were bombarded daily with new challenges. TV and radio brought those challenges to our doorstep — immediately. The rate of change was too rapid. The "domino theory" was not only a threat in Vietnam. One change will simply lead to another one, and every church struggled with the same fear. Some left the church because it was too slow to adapt. Others left because it was changing too fast. It was a tough time for leadership.

I think those were the years when I began to gain an appreciation for what it meant to lead an organization. How can an organization have competing convictions? This struggle has remained with me throughout my own career as a church leader. And, I guess, it will be there for the generations to come.

Exposure to Mennonite Understandings of Non-violence, Pacifism, and Non-resistance

One of the important teachings in Mennonite churches that has stuck for 500 years is pacifism. Although the sixteenth century Anabaptist movement was complex, and not all Anabaptists were non-violent, this conviction is one that has been sifted out of the complexity of our historical roots.

When I was young, it was not called pacifism or non-violence. It was called non-resistance. This was because in the King James Version of the Bible (which was the one used in our churches then), Jesus tells us: "…resist not evil…" (Mt. 5:39). One of the ways where this teaching was relevant was during time of war. Would young Mennonite men take up guns and bombs to kill the enemy? Or would they "resist not evil"? Thousands of Mennonites through the centuries had not taken up weapons. Some had been persecuted for this. Others had joined the war efforts, and they were often not very welcome in the church when they came home.

I was born during the last months of World War II. When I was a child, there was the Korean War, and in the 1960s there was the brutal war in Vietnam. So, war surrounded me in my childhood. But I heard of only one young man from Greenfarm who had enlisted in the military effort. It was assumed we would not enlist.

Yet, I never heard strong teaching about this in our church. I did hear our bishop say at one point that non-resistance was good, but when it came to communism "we had to bare our fists." In other words, the threat of communism was enough to soften our stance on non-resistance. When I was about fourteen years old (1959), some of the leaders in our church must have been concerned about this question. One day, my parents said they wanted me to come to a church meeting with them on a weekday evening. This was strange. They didn't invite my sisters, who were two and four years older than I was. This had not happened before. It was a mystery to me, and I was interested. So we went to our church.

There I discovered that the Mennonite churches in the region had invited a guest speaker, Mr. Plett. I believe he was a Mennonite of a different denomination from the Steinbach area. All these clues amplified a sense of how special it was to be there. Mr. Plett had been invited to come and explain why Mennonites don't go to war; why they are non-resistant. Other young people were there too along with many parents. I remember sitting with my parents (a rare experience) in the front row of the balcony (also rare). And there we listened to Mr. Plett. He seemed young to me; he had a very interesting and, I think, compelling talk. It was not a sermon. It was more like a heart-to-heart talk. I wasn't used to that from my ministers. He seemed like a very nice man, and I listened carefully to his presentation. Many of the questions I had in my mind seemed to find adequate answers.

As I look back now, I am convinced that Mr. Plett was a very important piece of the educational puzzle of my life. I accepted what he said, perhaps naively, and it has stayed with me. This experience has also convinced me that such special events can play a significant difference in the lives of young people and their parents. It has convinced me of the importance of the art of good teaching. Maybe it is in part why I decided to become a teacher, I'm not sure. But I know I am grateful for Mr. Plett, and I am thankful for whoever it was in our local church who thought it was a good idea to invite him.

Encountering Death

As I reflect on my early experiences, I am struck by the multiple occasions I came face-to-face with death. Some of these were stark and deeply disturbing for me as a young lad. The clarity of my memory suggests that these encounters impacted me significantly, but it's difficult to pinpoint in exactly what ways.

The first encounter I had was during the polio epidemic in the early 1950s. I was seven at the time. I saw the concern on my parents' faces. I heard them talk about various people I didn't know, but in quiet, almost whispering ways, and I knew it was serious. I remember my parents cutting back some visiting, but I don't know what else was implemented to prevent the spread of the disease. Then my cousin — who was just a bit older than I was — got the disease and died. I remember what a shock that was in the extended family. We all went to the funeral. I think it was the first time I saw a dead person in a coffin, and I saw the coffin being buried. Then our neighbour boy, also a bit older than I, died. With two young children dying very close by, I could sense more concern in our home.

We heard of many others who got the disease, but not everyone died. Some were paralyzed and required crutches or wheelchairs all their lives. I remember one young man who was taken to Winnipeg and put in an "iron lung," something I could not fathom or understand. I learned later it was a big tank that breathed for him because his lungs had been paralyzed. He remained in that "lung" all his life. I also remember Dr. Salk inventing the vaccine. People breathed a sigh of relief. Later, however, it was discovered that in the testing phase, some of the vaccine was tainted and actually paralyzed more persons. This is an important lesson as I am writing during the Covid-19 pandemic when many are anxious and rushing to get a vaccine out without significant testing.

A few years later, when I was about ten or so, my good friend, Billy, drowned in the watering hole on their farm. Again, the community was shocked. In our country school, we practiced a song to sing at the funeral. I still remember some of the lyrics:

> *Winter now is over and the spring is on its way;*
> *often do the storm clouds gather;*
> *from his throne in heaven God is watching one and all,*
> *He will ever care for you.*
> *After the clouds, the sun is always shining;*
> *after the storm the sky will all be blue.*
> *God has prepared a rosy-tinted lining;*
> *after the clouds, it's waiting to shine through.*

I remember the people sobbing as we sang and after we finished. I was old enough to understand the symbolic connection to the tragedy. It was a sad time for the entire community.

When I was twelve, one of my favourite uncles was killed in a tragic car accident. He was replacing a flat tire on the shoulder of the highway when a vehicle struck him. He left a large family of thirteen children. The younger of these cousins were very close to me. It was a tragic event. Fortunately, some of the older siblings were already old enough to keep the farm operation going. The funeral was large and sad.

Shortly after that came the rheumatic fever epidemic. Again, the results were bad. Many people I knew contracted the disease, including my brother, who was hospitalized and in recovery for most of six months. I don't remember as many dying from the disease, but its impact on the health of people was dramatic.

In 1959 when I was fourteen, my seventeen-year-old sister got sick one day. She was taken to the Winkler Hospital and died two days later. She was a healthy, vibrant girl who was gone very quickly. I don't think we ever knew exactly what took her away, but it was related to pneumonia and a respiratory illness. I remember going to the hospital room with my siblings and parents when she had already passed away. It was a heart-wrenching experience to see her there. I remember the day of the funeral in Winkler, I think it was a Saturday afternoon. When we got into the vehicle to drive to the cemetery for the burial, I noticed some people in town were mowing lawns, some were walking, some went into grocery stores, some were riding bikes. I remember becoming very angry: how was it possible for all these people to pretend that life was normal when my sister had died and it was anything but normal? It felt insensitive to me. I remember my brother-in-law, a large, husky man, crying at the cemetery. When we walked away from the burial site, he said to me with tears in his eyes: "This just isn't fair; it isn't fair."

When I was eighteen and had just graduated from high school, I was looking forward to the summer. My mother had been taken to the hospital with another concern for her heart. My dad told my sister and me that this time it seemed more serious. He looked concerned. A few days later, my sister, our father, and I were having a light lunch. The telephone rang, and my dad went to answer. He came back and in a broken voice said: "She's gone. She died." He sat down at the table and sobbed. I had never seen that before. My sister went over and put her arm over his shoulders and hugged him. I had never seen that before either. I didn't know what to do, so I just sat there. After a bit, my father said we needed to go to the hospital. Again, we went into her room with the body still in bed. Relatives began to come, and I remember how good it felt to have others come and be with us — especially with my dad. She was fifty-nine years old when she died.

There were other deaths that I experienced and remember vividly. My oldest sister's youngest brother-in-law, who was exactly my age, died in a tragic vehicle accident when I was fourteen. He was crushed by a vehicle driven by his older brother. Both my Suderman grandparents died when I was young: grandmother when I was nine, grandfather when I was thirteen.

I should say something about how funerals were conducted in those days. The body was embalmed and made to look as "alive" as possible. The deceased person was dressed in their Sunday best. The congregation was asked to rise. The service started with the family of the deceased person walking in behind the coffin. Everyone was seated, and then the coffin was opened in front of the congregation. That was always a time of increased sobbing and crying. Then the service was conducted with singing, prayer, Bible reading, reading of the obituary, and the sermon. Then came the "viewing." While the family sat in the front pews, the people walked slowly past the coffin for one last look. Some stopped to touch the body. Most wept. They would then walk past the family and shake hands with the family members, sometimes hugging them. It was difficult for the family, but therapeutic, I think. This human death march lasted a long time because most of these funerals were very large.

The people were invited to join the family for the short trip to the cemetery for burial and then back to the church for a funeral lunch. There was a short committal service at the graveside. The family then went back to the church where the lunch was served by shifts, and everyone got a chance again to express their condolences to the family. It was an extended time of very public, communal grieving.

As I recount this, I realize how things have changed. Today, our children seldom see the corpse at the hospital, the funeral home, or the church. Often the bodies are cremated before anyone has a chance to see, touch, or be with them. The coffins today are generally not opened during the service. We see pictures of the person alive, but we don't see them dead.

I think the experiences we had with death were helpful because there was no attempt to hide anything. It was clear to me, even as a small child, that the person was dead. It wasn't that they had "passed," that they "were in a better place," or that they were "alive with Jesus." To us it was clear that they were dead, and that needed to sink in before other things could be said. We had a clear sense of the finality of death. It was a sad moment. We did not pretend that nothing much of consequence had happened. It seems to me that the opportunities for public expressions of grief, trauma, and sadness were important. Also important were the public opportunities to express condolences, to sing together, and hear the prayers of the church.

My experiences with death did not stop at the age of eighteen, but I will stop here. There is something about how a community processes death that is instructive in how a community lives. Both death and life need to be handled with integrity and sensitivity. Both are God-given aspects of being human. In both, there can be visible expressions of God's love for each one.

II
Young Adult Life

31 Baptism candidates, 1962; Irene is 1st on right in second row; Jack 5th from right in back row. Ministers from left to right: Frank Letkeman, Jacob M. Pauls, Jacob Stobbe, Wilhelm Peters.

Baptism and Communion

The tradition in our church was that young people would get baptized. I say this was a tradition although it wasn't supposed to be that. It was supposed to be a personal decision made independently by each person. And, I think, in many ways it was that. But the personal decision clearly was influenced by tradition.

What were the dynamics of the tradition? Perhaps the most important key was that we could not have a church wedding, married by our minister, unless we were baptized. And so baptism had a lot of "collateral considerations." It wasn't only that I wanted to make a public declaration that I wanted to be a disciple of Jesus in community, but the other issues, such as marriage, were connected to my decision.

So, once we were between sixteen and nineteen years old, we began to think seriously about baptism. It was a family and community expectation. The communal hope was that young people would be baptized before graduating from high school. It was almost taken for granted. Yet, not entirely. There were some peers who decided not to get baptized, and chose to be married in other churches. My oldest sister got married in a different church, not because she wasn't baptized, but because her fiancé was not. I remember my mother being displeased about the rigidity of our bishop on that issue.

So in my Grade 11 year, I decided to be baptized. This had some implications. It meant that all those who wished the same were put into a special Sunday School class for at least six months. We were led through a little book of questions about the Christian faith, and given answers to these questions. This book was called a "catechism."

The catechism we used was published in High German. I think it was first published in Elbing (Prussia), a part of Germany, in 1778. The catechism had many questions, but we had to focus on twenty-four, with corresponding answers. The idea was that understanding the answers to these foundational questions was necessary and sufficient to be considered ready for baptism. We had to memorize the answers. And so every Sunday, the teacher would ask us a question, and we had to get up and publicly recite the answer to prove that we had done our homework. There was very little, if any, teaching about these answers. It was assumed that by memorizing the answers we understood, and we were doctrinally ready for baptism and for church membership. It was a bad assumption, but so it was.

Baptism was connected to church membership. One could not have one without the other. So the decision to be baptized was also a decision to become members of the church. This was all very serious business.

By the time the twenty-four weeks were over, it was assumed that we could recite — publicly, in German — the answers to all the questions. Two weeks before the baptisms were to be held, there was a special congregational meeting on a Sunday evening. At this meeting, all the baptism candidates were asked to be present. We (thirty-one of us) sat in the front pews of the full church. The ministers and deacons sat on the platform. They would get up in turn and read one of the questions from the catechism. They would then address the question to one of the candidates. That person then needed to get up and recite the answer — all of this in High German. The pressure was significant. Nobody wanted to mess up the answer, but some candidates were tongue-tied or blanked-out by the pressure and couldn't begin, or didn't remember. The ministers and deacons were kind. They provided just enough clues so the candidate could get through the answer. I remember getting it all right. My parents were proud.

Two weeks later, on Sunday morning, we were baptized. One by one we were invited to the stage, we knelt, and the bishop would pour water on our heads while the baptismal formula was recited: "I baptize you in the name of the Father, the Son, and the Holy Ghost." The bishop would then lean down, take our hand, and help us to our feet. He would then recite the next part of the formula: "I warmly welcome you as a bother (sister) into membership of the church. May God richly bless you and make you a blessing." And we could go back and sit down.

Baptisms traditionally took place on Pentecost Sunday, and Irene (my future wife) and I were both in the same baptismal class on June 10, 1962. The church service followed.

On that same Sunday evening, there was a solemn celebration of the Lord's Supper. This was the first time for the candidates to take part in or to be present during the Lord's Supper. We were celebrating our commitment as full, disciplined members of the congregation. The words of Paul were read. The bread, in little pieces, was distributed. We had been instructed by our parents prior to the service as to what to anticipate, as we had never seen this done before. We each needed to take a clean, white handkerchief along in our pockets. Then, when the bread was passed, we held out our hand covered by the clean handkerchief. The deacon would place the bread on the handkerchief. We were to look into the deacon's eyes and nod our heads slightly. When he nodded back, we knew that we were approved to eat the bread. We all waited for the signal to eat together.

The wine was passed around in a large, common cup starting with the first person in each row. That person would sip from the cup, take his/her white handkerchief and rub the place where their lips had been. He/she would then pass the cup to the next person. The same gesture of corresponding eye contact and nods were used for drinking of the cup.

Perhaps I need to say a word more about the eye contact and the nod. Mennonites, in those days, understood the Lord's Supper to be an expression of the believing and committed community that was symbolized by baptism. They took seriously the ideas expressed by the Apostle Paul in I Corinthians 11:27-29. There the apostle teaches that prior to participating in the Lord's Supper, each member is to "examine" his/her conduct and relationship with his/her brothers and sisters. Was there animosity? Was forgiveness needed with someone? Were things all right between you and the Body? Paul says that we should not participate in an "unworthy manner." And if this reconciliation homework had not been completed, we should not participate. He continues to say that if we eat and drink "without discerning the body" we eat and drink judgement on ourselves. The assurance that we had done our reconciliation homework before the Lord's Supper was symbolized by the eye contact and the discerning nods. These were signals that, yes, I did my homework, and, yes, I accept your discernment. With that, the Supper could be enjoyed in a "worthy manner."

Pentecost Sunday 1962 was a special day. It gave us a solemn sense of identity with the Body of the Church. We had publicly witnessed to our decision to be Jesus' disciple and now had the "rights and responsibilities" of church membership. We had signalled mutual "worthiness" to each other. The liturgy was embedded in our beings. Irene and I, to this day, look each other in the eye and give a nod — indiscernible to others, I'm sure — as we participate in communion services. We sometimes lament that this significant symbol of reconciled solidarity and the process of discerning the Body has been lost in our celebrations of the Lord's Supper.

Courtship and Marriage: I Don't Know What She Saw in Me

I was a young, raw, crude farm boy from a poor family. Irene was a suave, sophisticated, Winkler town girl from a family of some means. My parents were farmers; Irene's parents were businesspeople with farming on the side. I wanted to learn more because I wanted to know more. Irene was more focused on learning for vocational purposes. She wanted to be a nurse.

Irene's graduation as a Licensed Practical Nurse, 1964

Certainly, there was no social mingling between my parents and Irene's parents, even though both were in the same church. My father was a *Vorsaenger* (song chooser) and her mother was the organist. Irene and I grew up in the same church, although I did not attend Sunday School — which was for town kids — and I did not interact with her there. We attended the same youth activities, but connected to very different circles, so we didn't really notice each other very much. We sang in the same church choir, but again, that made no difference in knowing each other. She was the well-trained star and beloved soprano who was famous far and wide for her amazing solo rendition of *The Holy City* during advent every year, which she always sang to a packed church. I was a backbench tenor striving to imitate the good singer beside me. We were baptized on the same day, but the group was large and there was no significant personal connection.

We attended the same high school, but not in the same grade. She had her circles and I had mine. On weekends, my friends and I did what Winkler area young people did: we drove up and down Main Street while the girls walked up and down the sidewalks. The key was to catch someone's eye or to see some signal of interest in each other — perhaps a giggle or a wave. If so, we'd stop and talk — awkwardly — and sometimes the girls would get into the car, and we would go to the drive-in for an ice cream soda or cone. Irene was not one of the girls on the sidewalk, and there would have been no chance of interaction even if I would have been interested.

It was after high school when I was taking a one-year teacher training course in Winnipeg that my connection with Irene first began. She too was in Winnipeg taking a one-year licensed practical nursing course at the community college. It was my older sister who mentioned to me at one point that I should ask Irene out for a ride. I'm not sure how she knew because the two were not particularly close friends. But, I decided there was nothing to lose. I did have my father's 1952 Ford pickup truck to go to choir practice with, so I asked her if we could go for a ride. She was interested — I don't know why — and said yes. We drove to the neighbouring town and ordered French fries at a restaurant. That was the winter of 1964.

We began seeing each other more regularly: sometimes in Winkler, sometimes in Winnipeg. In January of 1965 it was time for a further step. Even though we were both still young — she twenty, I nineteen — we decided to get married. The tradition in those days was that the potential groom needed to request permission and blessing from the potential bride's parents, so we did, and her parents gave us their blessing.

Neither my father (mother had died when I finished high school) nor Irene's parents were particularly enthused with the idea. They thought we were too young and inexperienced. I also think that my future as a schoolteacher was not particularly inspiring for Irene's parents. But they were all gracious. Upon seeing our firm convictions to do this, they began to get on board, and then got excited about the marriage.

Jack and Irene Suderman wedding.

We were married on a Sunday afternoon, August 1, 1965, in the Winkler Bergthaler Church — our childhood church. Irene's father, being a very well known businessperson in Winkler, had invited virtually everyone he met, including the entire congregation. There were in excess of 500 people at the wedding, and we received piles and piles of gifts.

Signing the register with officiating pastor, John R. Friesen

The organization of the wedding itself was relatively simple. We needed to invite ministers: and we invited one to do a German message and one to speak in English. Pastor Friesen, who had been our youth pastor, enacted the ceremony and the vows. The women of the church took care of the food. The wedding service was followed by the traditional meal (*faspa*), and folks had to eat in shifts. In the evening, folks were invited to Irene's parents' home where the tradition of opening gifts would take place. The whole big basement was full of people and gifts. We opened gifts till almost midnight, with the onlookers — especially the women — duly oohing and aahing every time the wrapping came off another set of linens or one more toaster.

Another tradition in those days was that friends of the groom or brothers of the bride would play a trick on the newly-wedded couple. They would do something with the honeymoon car — in our case a beautiful 1953 two-toned, two-door Chevrolet. I had been able to buy this, my first car, for $350 with the help of a loan from my father. Sometimes the trick was old cheese on the engine to create an awful smell. Sometimes it was flattening the tires. Sometimes the classic tin cans and such were tied behind. We had made arrangements with a friend we could trust to hide the car in his garage on the farm. At a given signal, he would bring the car to the house, we would rush out, say goodbye, and race off before anything could happen.

This ploy worked, but Irene's brother and his cronies decided to chase us. Luckily, we had decided to go into the USA for our honeymoon. They followed us all the way to the border but didn't come through. We were finally alone. Our honeymoon took us to Detroit Lakes, Duluth, Thunder Bay and back to Winnipeg. We got back in time for me to begin my new job as a teacher in a small country school close to Winkler, and Irene would work as a nurse in the Winkler Hospital.

We have now been married fifty-five years. As we review the past and share our memories, we agree that we made the best decision as young people. We have had a rich and good marriage. We are blessed with a very fine family, and we love our grandchildren and are proud of each one. God has been good, just as the minister at our wedding told us. We are grateful.

Navigating University Life: My Communist Professor and My Faith

After a year of teaching in a country school and Irene working as a nurse in Winkler, we decided it was time for me to go to university in Winnipeg. I had been taking summer and evening courses, but I wanted to finish the degree. So, in the summer of 1966 we moved to Winnipeg. We found a tiny apartment right across the street from the hospital where Irene would be working and walking distance to my university. We moved into our two-room apartment on the second floor.

I needed two years to finish a bachelor of arts degree with a major in geography and minor in political science. I found that to be a helpful combination. Irene worked the different shifts the hospital demanded. She worked primarily on the maternity ward.

Jack's graduation with a BA degree (1968)
from the University of Winnipeg.

These two years were good years. We had good friends, who were also in similar situations. And we connected with the church in Winnipeg.

Two things stand out for me in my undergraduate university experience. One was that a number of my peers from Winkler, also studying at one of the universities in Winnipeg, were not able to adapt the new information they were learning to the understanding of faith that they learned in Winkler. Many left the church, and faith seemed to be archaic and not the place to be. I too struggled. I had a leaning toward cynicism, and I became aware that there was much information I had never received. I struggled with finding my way. Luckily, our good friend, Bill, was a traditional and very stubborn Christian — at least as I saw it at that time. We disagreed on most everything faith related, but we were very good friends and spent much time together. We had hours and hours of arguments and discussions, attempting to make sense of what we were learning with what we had known till then. Bill was able to twist and turn and somehow adapt — badly, I often thought — his learnings so that he could hang on to his faith. I think it was his — often illogical — determination to hang on that saved me from following my peers into agnostic tendencies. I am still grateful for him. It was an ironic case of disagreement that led to a deepening friendship and, in the end, continuing faith for me. I sometimes think that I was evangelized by error. But I am grateful for his steadfast influence and his solid friendship. Bill died too early. Not long ago, I was invited to speak at his funeral in Winkler. I had thanked him often before, but there I was able to publicly thank him for his influence on me.

The other clear memory is of my communist professor of geography. He was a tiny man with robust energy, and a very dynamic teacher. He questioned some of the things I had always assumed to be bedrock. For example, he made an extended argument for why the British land survey system in western Canada was at fault for slow and inefficient growth of the Canadian economy. His compelling point was that if Canada would have accepted the French system of long-lots rather than the British system of square miles, life on the prairies would have been much better. I won't go into details. But he was critiquing something that I had always assumed was simply a given. Who would think of critiquing the survey system of a country? He was very passionate about that point, and it opened a whole new dynamic for me. It made me realize that what is today, is the product of decisions that somebody made yesterday. There are no accidents. What we have today is the fruit of something yesterday.

This point — as simple as it seems now — was mind-blowing for a farm boy from Winkler. I could hardly imagine that my childhood farm with the mile-roads on each side could have been imagined differently. But this professor did, and he explained how it would actually have been better. It allowed me to appreciate the world in a new way.

I am grateful for these university years, and for the friends that helped us on the way. I am grateful for Irene who paid the bills and allowed me to finish that first degree with no debt. And I'm grateful for the background in geography and political science that I accumulated. Only later would I discover how important these were also for the study of the Bible and theology.

Killing at the Mennonite Credit Union: Face to Face with Money

During my university years, we attended a local Mennonite church in Winnipeg. A friend and I became the youth sponsors: volunteer positions to provide some structure and programming to the youth of the congregation.

In those days, it was quite important to us all that we had a Mennonite credit union in Winnipeg. It functioned like a cooperative. Mennonites could save their money and trust that it was used for good, ethical, and community-building purposes. We, of course, had no money to invest, but it was a good feeling to know that my church was part of such a significant effort.

One day the news lit up with the report that there had been an attempted robbery at the credit union, and that two robbers had been killed, and one robber badly wounded. As it turned out, the wounded one was relegated to a wheelchair for the rest of his life. This was big news, but the details were still to come. As information slowly oozed out from the Winnipeg Police reports, it became evident that the police had forewarning of the day and hour of the planned robbery. They had informed the credit union manager and had made a plan. They allowed public access to continue, and the police planted heavily-armed plain-clothes officers around the front and back entrances, inside, and some on telephone poles nearby. These were to serve as early warning systems. They wanted to catch the thieves in the act of robbery rather than only in conspiracy to rob. So they put the public at great risk and prepared to "take out" the robbers once they were in the act of robbing the credit union.

This sounded significantly "un-Mennonite" to some of us. How could it be that guarding our money was worth two lives and one severely wounded? The plan was predicated not on protecting our money, but on catching the robbers in action, killing them if necessary. One thing seemed clear to us: as Mennonites we needed to denounce not only the police action, but also the plan they had put in place. They had time; they could have come up with a plan that was safer for the public and the employees, and that was designed to save life rather than take it.

We felt we were on solid "Mennonite" ground, and that our community would rush to our support. So, a few of us wrote an open letter indicating these views and asking the credit union board to issue an apology to the public in Winnipeg. The plan was to publish this letter in the *Winnipeg Free Press*. But, we thought, it would be better if the letter would come from a recognized group — like our church council — rather than a spontaneous gathering of like-minded individuals. So, we asked for a meeting with the council. To our surprise and shock, the credit union board of directors beat us to the punch. A letter had already been drafted publicly congratulating the Winnipeg Police Department for their risky, prompt and effective action, and thanking them for their decisive support. Furthermore, we noted that a highly respected man from our congregation was a member of the credit union board.

It was then we realized that this wouldn't be a simple discussion. We decided not to send the letter to the newspaper, but sent it instead to our church council because we felt it needed significant discussion at the congregational level. Nothing further happened. There never was further discussion. We were not invited to the council for an airing of the issue. There was simply silence.

This was a great disappointment, and it punctured a hole in the trust I had placed in the common testimony of church. It also nurtured some negative tendencies I already had about the church. I had never considered myself as a young radical. I thought we were articulating our common faith in the face of an incident relevant to all of us. I thought we would be applauded. It was an important lesson — or series of lessons for me. One lesson was that I understood more fully the power of money. Was our money worth these killings? Apparently, yes. It also taught me about the power of people who have money, including our fellow church members. Most of all it taught me that experience in the church would always, by definition, involve experience with people. This meant that the nature and nurture of all the members would always need to be on the table. It was a reminder that the church is in the world, but it is also of the world in more ways than we sometimes want to admit. Lastly, it taught me that the need for ongoing Christian education of all congregational members is a never-ending task of the church. These were valuable lessons that stuck with me.

My Exposure to Biblical/Theological Debate: Learning as a Teacher

When I finished my BA from the University of Winnipeg, I received an unexpected call from the principal of a Mennonite middle and high school in Winnipeg. Would I be interested in teaching Grades 7 and 8 social studies, Grades 10 and 11 history, and Grade 10 geography? How could I say no? I was looking for work, and the teaching assignments were more or less connected to what I was studying. I had also begun a bachelor of education degree with a major in history. So, with studies in geography, political science, and history, this offer seemed very good to me.

I checked with my dad, who discouraged me. He said: "You're only twenty-three years old. You have no experience with city kids. They will drive you out of the classroom." In spite of his advice, I took the job. Little did I know that in the five years in that school I would be the primary learner. The teaching went well, and I enjoyed it very much. I think most students liked me as a teacher.

I learned much from my students. One day, a suave Grade 10 student walked into my class, sniffed around, and asked: "Were the Grade 9s in here last?" I said, yes, why do you ask? "It smells like puberty," he said.

In addition to the classroom, I organized the senior classes into a curling league. Every Friday at 4 pm during the winter months we would all head to the curling rink to play. It was fun. I also accompanied the senior choir on tours to churches.

A big surprise for me, however, was that the faculty room became a very important classroom for me. I was a farm boy. I had never had any formal theological or biblical training. We didn't go to Sunday school. I didn't go to a private high school. I didn't go to the Bible school in Altona. I didn't enrol in the Bible college in Winnipeg. I went straight from high school to teacher's college to university. In the faculty room, I was surrounded by Bible college and seminary-trained graduates as teaching peers. It was a time of extreme social and political turbulence. It was, after all, still the 1960s and the early 1970s. The struggle to make our Mennonite faith relevant for the current situation was very alive. My peers were very creative. I think thousands of ideas were tested and passionately argued. Each one connected in some way to our Anabaptist traditions, our reading of the Bible, and our theological reflection. We were always sorry when the bells rang calling us back to the classroom.

I was more than intrigued — I was mesmerized. I had not had this kind of systematic, yet spontaneous exposure to the Bible, theology, or our church's history before. My carpooling companion was one of the more creative minds. He was at one end of the spectrum, and I had the opportunity of thirty minutes a day extra personal tutoring. These folks could be skeptical, critical, and cynical. But their passion for the relevance of their history and faith — if rightly understood — never wavered. They were deeply embedded, wholly committed, and thoroughly convinced they could make this all work. They more than sparked my interest. They ignited a passion in me that I didn't know was there.

After five years of this intense training, Irene and I were ready to take our next step. And that would need to somehow formalize the theological/biblical training I had received in the faculty room. The location seemed to be a no-brainer: it would be our seminary in Elkhart, Indiana. While they offered only master's level courses and I had not had any undergraduate theological studies, my colleagues all convinced me that I was capable of handling what would come my way there. So, in 1973 we made our plans to move to Elkhart for two years of study.

Those years consolidated our conviction that the presence and the work of the church was vital in God's plan to redeem the world. We both participated in weekly small group meetings, which nurtured our souls, fostered lifelong friendships, and allowed us to process our personal agenda. Those years changed our lives in ways we didn't understand until much later.

We are grateful for these colleagues and the opportunities we had to prepare better for the work and ministry that lay ahead. They pointed us to a path that we wanted to travel but didn't know was there.

Learning to be Parents

Marriage and then having children are surely the biggest and most important game-changing experiences we can imagine. At least, so it has been with us. We have had the amazing fortune of bringing three sons into this world: Bryan in 1969; Derek in 1972; and Andrew in 1978. The first two were born during my time as a teacher in Winnipeg, and Andrew was born during our time in Rosthern, Saskatchewan, where we moved after seminary in Elkhart. I was invited to be the principal of the Mennonite high school there.

We made some important decisions during those years. One was that if we were going to be parents, we wanted to be good parents — as good as we knew how. It may sound strange to say this, but I remember having significant discussions about this with Irene. One sub-product of that discussion was that we would try — if circumstances permitted — to be a one-income family. Irene was willing and ready to give up her job as a nurse, at least for the time being.

Most of the credit of parenting belongs to Irene. She was a positive pillar. While I worked for a salary — almost day and night — and needed to travel a lot, she was providing daily care, guidance, and stability to the boys and to our home. She, of course, also got involved in a multitude of volunteer responsibilities, but our boys were our priority.

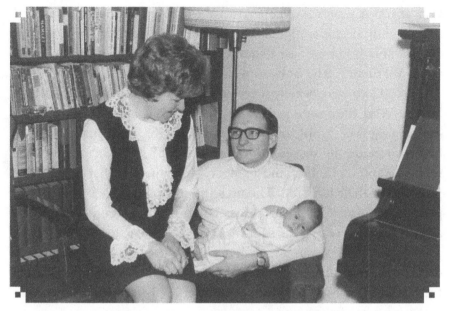

New parents with son, Bryan, 1969.

The one-income decision had various components. The most important was the stability and parental presence it would provide for raising our children. Another was an expression of our convictions to the world. We were living in changing times when two-income families were rapidly becoming the norm. That brought other challenges and dynamics that we didn't want to face. I remember being impacted by one of my seminary professors. In a class where we were engaging the issues of world over-population and Christian responsibilities in light of that, and in a context of new options for birth control, one of the students dared asked the professor: "So how do you justify having a larger family than most?" His reply was: "The world needs more children like mine." At the time, it seemed like a boastful and arrogant comment — and maybe it was. But with time, I learned to understand it as a challenge to parenthood. If we were going to be parents, then we should do our best to make that a good thing for others and for the world. It was a challenge we began to embrace more consciously and more conscientiously.

Our boys were a constant source of joy and learning for us. They were normal kids. They never lacked energy nor creative ideas. They were also, at times, a source of concern that tugged at our heartstrings and left us with sleepless nights. I remember our decision to leave our comfortable home in Saskatchewan and go to Latin America (more about that later). The boys were eleven, eight, and two at the time. The oldest two were heavily invested in Rosthern's favourite past-time: hockey. And they were getting to the point where they were good; showing signs of significant potential. One player from our small town had even made the successful leap to the NHL. This inspired all the rest — players, coaches, and parents — to imagine that it might be possible for their boys too. The pressure to produce good players was persistent and profound. Our decision to pull out our boys and provide a Latin American experience for them was not understood. Some of our acquaintances felt it was almost like child abuse. How dare we make a decision that would most certainly curtail any promise of them reaching the NHL? At times we felt guilty. Were we simply feeding our own egos at the expense of our boys?

Irene and I had had some serious conversations about what legacy we wanted to leave to our boys, and this impacted our parenting style and our parental decisions. We became more convinced that, given the complex and changing world we were experiencing — these were the 1970s, after all — we wanted our boys to become "world citizens" in ways that were more conscious than what we had experienced in our lives. We focused on four things we wanted to give our boys. One was that we wanted them to know and experience a different culture — not just as tourists, but by immersion. We were convinced that deeply knowing another culture was the best way to understand our own. Second, we wanted them to become fluent in another language. Language, we knew, is a window into the soul of culture, and we felt a responsibility to provide that. Third, we wanted them to experience the other side of affluent North America. We were not wealthy by any North American measuring stick, but we knew we were affluent when compared to billions of people in the world. We wanted our boys not only to taste this difference, but to experience it deeply. And fourth, we wanted them to experience profoundly that their parents tried to "walk the talk" in terms of faith, church, discipleship, and being "Mennonite" or "Anabaptist." We hoped that wherever we went and whatever we did they would see and feel our commitment to the ways of God as we understood them from our theological lenses.

What exactly these foci would mean for our boys, we did not know. We only trusted that they would be helpful as their own lives unfolded.

I will not comment here on the success or failure of our parental idealism. We know that parenting is too complex to fixate on particular components of it. What I can say is that it was helpful for us as parents to have an articulated framework for at least some aspects of parenting. I can also say that we did our best, even in the midst of a thousand missteps, mistakes, and blunders in the process. The last word on all of this must rest with the boys. They are the only experts in assessing our parenting efforts. We are, however, grateful for and proud of each of them.

III

Consolidating Life and Vocation

Close Encounter with John G. Diefenbaker: Making History – Apparently

I was the principal of Rosthern Junior College from 1975-80. It was a Mennonite residential school founded in 1905 by early pioneers in Saskatchewan with a long tradition of what was referred to as "education with a plus." Our five years there were dynamic, challenging, and growing years for me. I worked with an excellent faculty and staff, and added more very fine faculty as the years marched on. My time there gave me much-needed experience and once-in-a-lifetime moments.

The school was founded in 1905, so we were approaching the seventy-fifth anniversary of the life of the school. In 1978, the board of directors began to organize some special, commemorative events to celebrate this important milestone. Among other things, Dr. Frank H. Epp, a noted Canadian and Mennonite historian, was commissioned to write a definitive history of the school. We were glad that he accepted the challenge. Traditionally, the June grad weekend had grown to be a big thing at the college. In addition to the graduation service, there was always a major musical drama production, and this school year there would also be a full-length choral production. These productions were of high, almost professional, level. They were showcases for our music, drama, and fine arts departments. In addition to that, it was the weekend of the alumni reunions. Typically, several thousand people attended the various events, and June of 1979 would be no exception. Indeed, it would be the biggest ever.

We planned for this event for a year. One of the key decisions was who to invite as our guest speaker for the graduation service. After much discussion, it was decided to invite the former prime minister of Canada, the Honourable John G. Diefenbaker. There was good rationale for this decision. He had taught in a school in a Mennonite area close to Rosthern, is present political riding was Prince Albert, which included the town of Rosthern, and he had been a long-time friend of the Mennonites. It was also no secret that, politically, they were a friend to him.

So, we contacted Diefenbaker's office in September of 1978, a full nine months before the event. We invited him to give the convocation address on the Sunday afternoon in June. We didn't hear from his office for a long time. We were getting nervous. Finally, in mid-December we received a call from his office that he would not be able to make it because he had other responsibilities outside the country, I believe. So, we enacted Plan B. Given that Dr. Epp's commissioned book about the college would be published before June, we decided to invite him to be our speaker. He was delighted and accepted the invitation. Then we continued with other details of the planning.

All was well. Then, on Friday, June 23, 1979, two days before the graduation service, but with the musical, choral, and alumni activities already in full swing, I received a call in my office from the office of Mr. Diefenbaker. His aide informed me that Mr. Diefenbaker would be able to make it after all, that he was looking forward to giving his speech, and asked for details about when to arrive, and how the afternoon was planned. I was dumb-struck. Every detail of every service had been in place for weeks, if not months. Every responsibility had been assigned. All was in place and was already underway.

I did not have time to consult. I said as gently and as kindly as I could that I was very sorry, but it would not be possible. We had received a

"No" from his office, and we had made alternate arrangements. The aide was insistent that Mr. Diefenbaker really wanted to come, and would indeed be there. I indicated with gentle firmness that he was welcome, but that he would not be speaking because we had engaged another eminent speaker for the event. The aide asked about other options because Mr. Diefenbaker wanted to meet and greet the Mennonites. He asked whether he could hand out the diplomas on stage, and I said no, that too had already been organized. Then I suggested an alternative.

I suggested that if his primary interest was to meet and greet, he should come later in the afternoon on Saturday (the next day), when the alumni would have a massive BBQ before the grand evening production of the musical and the choral performance. I indicated that there would be well over a thousand people there, and it would be an ideal time for him to meet the people. I also offered that if he would like, we could introduce him at the beginning of the grand evening production, and he could then decide if he wished to stay for the lengthy three-and-a-half-hour production, or he could leave after his words of greeting. Given that Mr. Diefenbaker was a bit frail at the time and dealing with some health issues, his aide seemed to think that this might be doable. He asked how much time we would make available for his greetings, and I carefully explained what was happening that evening, and the extraordinary length of the program, but that we would be happy to give him five minutes at the beginning to greet our people. He agreed and indicated that they would come the next day — not for the BBQ, but only for the production. We scrambled to add one more chair in the sold-out space, and placed the chair beside Dr. Frank Epp's. We thought it would be good for a well-known Conservative and a well-known Liberal to enjoy the production together.

The next day, I was in my office a half hour before the evening production was to begin. Some students came running into my office saying that there was a large, black car outside and the occupants were asking for me. I went down to welcome the former prime minister. I walked up to the side of the car and the back window rolled down. There was Mr. Diefenbaker with a characteristic scowl (I should say glare) on his face.

I introduced myself, and he tersely invited me (better said, ordered me) to get into the front seat of the car because he wanted to speak with me. I obliged.

Mr. Diefenbaker didn't waste time and didn't mince words. He was furious. He indicated that "Never in the course of Canadian history has a former prime minister ever been limited to five minutes as an invited guest." He further stated that: "This is a scandal of large proportions. Mennonites will be infamous for daring to break protocol in such a dramatic fashion." I listened to his harangue (I've only quoted a small portion of what he said), and again, gently and softly apologized but indicated that we really could not make any changes. I reminded him that the message from his office had been that he was not coming, and that this indication of his presence was too late to make significant shifts to the program. But I did invite him in to greet the crowd. He said this was a great "insult." He said he had mentioned this insult to Prime Minister Trudeau, and Trudeau had replied: "It must be difficult to be a former prime minister." Then he went on for another lengthy speech (rant) about how Acadia University had given him an honorary doctorate because they appreciated his service and stature. He also indicated the Baptist University had invited him and had honoured him. This insult from the Mennonites would go down in history as the worst possible insult for a former prime minister. I again listened, again apologized, and again invited him inside. The production was about to begin.

He agreed, and his aide stepped out and went around to open the door for him. Mr. Diefenbaker was frail but walked slowly to the auditorium. The crowd was already gathered, ready to begin, and there were gasps of recognition as I took his arm and led him to the front. He pronounced to me that they would not stay for the production, but would only give his greetings and leave.

The aide and I helped him up the several steps to the stage. I went to the microphone and indicated that we were blessed to have a prominent visitor with us. I introduced him, indicating some of his significant achievements, and then I invited him to greet our Mennonite people. Mr. Diefenbaker walked over and took the microphone in his hand — away from the podium. Upon seeing the huge crowd before him, his countenance changed. There was no more sign of frailty. He spoke with energy and authority, without notes, for about twenty-five minutes. He waved to the crowd and signalled that he was ready to get off the stage. He received an exuberant ovation. His aide and I helped him off. I thanked him and wished him well, and they left.

I did not explain to the crowd that this was an unauthorized lengthening of a very long evening program. They took it in stride, as did the musicians, actors, conductors, and directors. We had a great evening.

I pondered this encounter and talked to my board of directors about it. I wondered how serious my politically naive guffaw had been, and whether indeed all Mennonites would forever more be tainted in the eyes of our governmental institutions. They assured me that I had handled the situation well, and that I had been the target of the wrath of Mr. Diefenbaker's unmitigated ego.

Mr. Diefenbaker died about seven weeks later, on August 16, 1979. His funeral train passed through Rosthern on the way to Prince Albert. I went out to salute him passing by. I couldn't help but wonder whether my historic political insult had in any way hastened his death. I had, however, also done some additional reading about him after the June encounter. I read that he was in an advancing state of dementia, and that he was known to do some strange things. I chalked up my experience with him to this latter evidence. Knowing this, however, did make his speech to the crowd even more remarkable. It was very good, delivered without notes. Thankfully, I have neither seen nor heard of any further evidence that the Canadian Mennonite image and reputation had been severely damaged. I am at peace. And I trust that Mr. Diefenbaker is also resting in peace.

The Decision: Latin America with the Mission Board

Our experience at the Associated Mennonite Biblical Seminaries in Elkhart, Indiana, was brief but very rich. For the first time in our lives, we were thrust into a theological learning community that was both ecumenical and global. We encountered fellow students from many parts of the world and from a variety of denominational backgrounds. All of us engaged in deepening our understanding of faith, doctrine, the Bible, theology, and history. Deep friendships were forged that continue to this day.

One of the persons we met was a missionary recruiting agent for the General Conference Mennonite Church mission board — The Commission on Overseas Mission (COM). He visited the campus several times searching out potential candidates for mission assignments. The Mennonite Central Committee (MCC) was also present at various intervals.

Both agencies had heard about us, and wanted to talk about possibilities. We were willing to talk, but reticent to commit to anything yet. Before the two years were up, however, Irene and I had made a firm decision that we wanted to go "somewhere, sometime," but the time was not yet ripe to do so. We did encourage both agencies, however, to stay in touch because at some point we would be ready. The agent, John, from COM took us up on this invitation.

We left seminary and headed for Saskatchewan where I had been invited as principal in the Mennonite College there. We dove into our new assignment and got involved in our new community. Our youngest son was born in Rosthern. John faithfully kept in touch at least twice a year. Each time he sketched different options that might be of interest to us. Each time we said: "Thank you, but not yet." After the third year we began to think more seriously about going somewhere as a live option. But not quite yet. We asked John to keep us informed, and he did.

We began to do some investigations of our own. We discovered an option with MCC that seemed to be tailor-made for us. Those were the days of the iron curtain, the enforced isolation of the Soviet Union and other communist bloc countries in Eastern Europe from the rest of the world. MCC was itching for some presence behind the iron curtain, but it was prohibited to do any overt Christian service there. So MCC came up with the idea of having someone enrol in a master's degree program at the university in Prague, Czechoslovakia. The assignment would be to live as a student, perhaps investigate some areas of MCC interest in the Eastern Bloc, and to relate to a local congregation simply as congregants.

This was very appealing to us, and we began to get excited about his option. Then Irene and I made another key decision to set a framework for our decision making. We decided two things: one, that when we went, we would go with MCC and not with COM; the other that we were open to going anywhere in the world except to Latin America. With this definitive framework, we continued to listen and watch.

The Prague assignment was attractive, so we applied to MCC. We heard nothing for a long time, and then received a letter indicating that we were not accepted because they could not send candidates with families into the Eastern Bloc. It had to be either single persons or a couple without children. We were disappointed.

Not long after that, John called again indicating that he had a new option he thought would be of interest to us. COM had received an invitation from a Baptist seminary in Cochabamba, Bolivia, to send a professor with Anabaptist convictions to teach Bible and theology at the seminary. It was a lovely setting for a family: live on campus with other student families, the boys could attend a good international school, and Irene was invited to teach music at the seminary and relate closely to the wives of the male students on campus. We would be the only Mennonites in this beautiful mountain city.

We listened carefully. It was, indeed, a good match. But what about our overarching decisions to go with MCC and not COM, and to avoid Latin America? This offer shattered both of the "definitive" decisions. We struggled with the invitation. In the end, we felt that we needed to acknowledge that we were ready to break our framework. We would go with COM to Latin America. As it turned out, it was an excellent decision. It was an invigorating environment for each one of us in the family. And, I think, we made significant contributions to the Baptist churches in Bolivia.

Our family arriving in Cochabamba, Bolivia, 1981.

In 2017, we were invited back to Cochabamba for a reunion. It had been thirty-two years since we left. To our surprise about forty ex-students and faculty members showed up. We spent a pleasant morning recounting memories and sharing what we had all learned. It was inspiring to hear the stories of these ex-students, now pastors and leaders.

We have often wondered, however, about our decision-making process. Where did we go wrong that we needed to do exactly the opposite of what we had decided to do? The best response is that God has a great sense of humour. We do what we can in our human condition, wisdom, and frailty, but God's Spirit sometimes guides us beyond what we can imagine. And, it seems, God smiles — maybe even laughs at us. But it is not a harsh laugh; it is playful and gentle. And it helps us laugh at ourselves too. And, perhaps, it helps us laugh with God.

Close Encounter with Dictator Garcia Meza: Sermon on the Mount or Silence in the Face of Brutality?

We arrived in Cochabamba, Bolivia, in June 1981. The country was in a high state of unrest. There had been several military coups that brought a brutal dictator, Luis Garcia Meza, to power. There was high inflation. Most things were unstable. We were there for the last three months of Meza's brutal rule. But the dictator that ousted him, Celso Torrelio, wasn't any better. He continued the brutal repression Meza's regime began.

I began teaching at the Baptist seminary in September. One of Meza's ongoing legacies was the prohibition he had implemented on some "prohibited and seditious" materials. The materials were not to be made available, read, or taught.

Baptist seminary in Cochabamba, Bolivia.

We were surprised to see Matthew 5-7 on the list of prohibited, seditious material. This is the section that is often referred to as Jesus' "Sermon on the Mount." In these chapters, Jesus outlines in brief form what it means to be a disciple of his. How could such a sermon be seditious? The added complexity for me, and for the seminary, was that I was scheduled to teach the Gospel of Matthew that semester. Baptists being Baptists lean toward obeying the government, seeing it as God's instrument for peace and order. Should we continue with the course? We identified several options. One was to ignore the order and simply teach the Gospel as we always would. This would be in direct defiance of a government order, something Baptists are hesitant to do. Another option would be to continue with the course but leap-frog over chapters 5-7. That way the course schedule would not be interrupted, and we would be obeying government orders. A third option would be to cancel the course.

These options were discussed at length at the faculty meetings. In the end, the faculty felt that we did not have the authority to make the decision. So we brought it to the seminary board. They too struggled with the answer. Finally, they decided that in this case, we simply needed to forge ahead with teaching the course, including chapters 5-7. As a foreign professor, there was the added risk of being seen as "intervening" in the internal politics of Bolivia, but I agreed to go ahead with the course.

In the first class, the president of the seminary came into my class to explain what the decision had been and why. He encouraged the students to study the Gospel diligently — including chapters 5-7 — and to pray for the welfare of the seminary and the country. I began the course asking the students to pay special attention to the content of chapters 5-7. I asked them to consider the following question: "Why do you think a brutal military dictator with all the power of the army and air force under his control would see this material as dangerous to his regime and power?"

We continued with the course. We examined chapters 5-7 verse by verse. When we finished I asked for their responses to the question I had asked. Why would this material be deemed dangerous, threatening, or seditious to a military dictator? To my surprise, the students were unanimous in their response: Garcia Meza was right. This material surely is dangerous for a regime such as his. If Bolivians were exposed to the material and begin to live according to the teachings found there, military dictatorships would crumble. It was a significant moment of learning. Some students recounted this experience thirty-two later as we shared memories of our time together.

Some of the seminary students in Cochabamba. All
are Quechua or Aymara indigenous students.

So what did we learn? For one, the Bolivian Baptists had deliberately
entered into a process of civil disobedience and intentionally disobeyed
a government policy. This was a new experience for them. Secondly, we
experienced anew the lesson of the early church recorded in Acts 5:28-
29. The apostles, led by Peter, were teaching in the plazas and streets
of Jerusalem. The authorities came by and said: "We gave you strict
orders not to teach in this name, yet here you have filled Jerusalem
with your teaching...." Peter and the apostles reply: "We must obey
God rather than any human authority." This experience in ancient
Jerusalem had become personal experience in Cochabamba in 1981.
It was a dramatic and sobering lesson. Third, we all learned again
how relevant an old text can be for new situations. The early church
and Luke (the writer of the Book of Acts) knew nothing about the
Bolivians in the twentieth century, and yet their experience seemed to
speak directly to them in Cochabamba. I think this was an important
lesson for these young, humble Quechua and Aymara church leaders
who were learning to be pastors. And it was an important lesson for
me as a novice seminary teacher with the mandate to make Anabaptist

perspectives of faith known and relevant for the Bolivian Baptist Church. Thankfully, there were no governmental repercussions. I don't know if we would have been ready to take the next steps of disobedience.

Playing Ecumenical Fastball: Evangelizing the Evangelists

We lived in Cochabamba, Bolivia for four years. It is a lovely, quaint, peaceful city, nestled into a valley in the Andes Mountains. It's climate was near perfect. It avoided the extreme heat and humidity of the lowlands, and the extreme cold of the windy, barren highlands. Indeed, it was so nice that the joke was that God calls a lot of missionaries and mission boards to Cochabamba. In some ways, this was true. Cochabamba was the primary headquarters of many Christian organizations, especially those from North America. There were the Wycliffe Bible Translators, The New Tribes Mission, the Baptists, the Church of God, the Mormons, and the Jehovah's Witnesses, to name just a few. This meant that there were high numbers of foreigners living in Cochabamba, especially from North America.

We settled into the small house on the seminary campus. Across the street from the seminary was an empty lot. It was not really a park, it simply hadn't yet been developed. We began to notice that every Saturday morning there was a group of Bolivian men who gathered there to play fastball. Their leader was a renowned local artist who also was the windmill pitcher for the team. Some had baseball gloves, others did not. They had one bat. But they seemed disciplined and serious about their outing. This was curious for us because Bolivia is not known for baseball, much less for fastball. But, given that I had enjoyed playing fastball in my adolescent, youth, and young adult life, I was attracted to their efforts.

Bryan, Derek, Andrew quickly fell in love with
Andean music and instruments.

One Saturday, our oldest son and I decided to edge closer and talk to
these men. They were thrilled that we stopped by and immediately
wanted to sign us up to play. We were not ready, but I did get to know
the leader (Jaime), and we became good friends. Frankly, the playing
was not high quality. They were beginners, but they liked the new sport
that Jaimie had introduced to them. Saturday after Saturday they would
play, usually between seven and thirteen men along with Bryan and I.

One Saturday, Jaimie approached me and asked if it would be possible
for me to bring a team to play against them. Knowing the many North
Americans from the various mission projects, I indicated that I thought
it would be possible. However, I knew that many North Americans'
national sport was baseball, and I was afraid that there would be a
significant mismatch in the ability of play. I suggested that perhaps it

would be a better idea if I invite a number for the next Saturday, but that we would choose teams and mix everybody up into two teams. That way there would be more and less experienced guys on each team, thus equalizing the strength of each team somewhat. Jaimie would not hear about this. He said they wanted to improve, and the only way they would improve would be to play against people that are better than them. He said it didn't matter if they lost. They wanted to learn by doing.

I contacted a number of mission houses, and the next Saturday we had more than enough to make a team. Many also brought additional balls, bats, and a catcher's mask. The excitement was high on both sides. I too was a windmill pitcher, and Bryan — thirteen years old at the time — was an excellent catcher. So, we took to the field with a full compliment of players.

We trounced them. I felt badly, but Jaimie continued to insist that this was important for their learning process.

They asked for another game the following Saturday. Our guys were only too happy to oblige. This developed into a routine. Those who could make it would play fastball on Saturday mornings. We had a broad mix of mission personnel represented, including, to our surprise, the young Mormon men whom we had seen on the streets with their white shirts and ties. They had told me that their supervisor was not in agreement with them "mixing" with us, but the mission community began to talk to each other like never before. We developed friendships with others. And we developed friendships with the Bolivians. The Saturday morning fastball became a tradition and continued for the entire four years we were there. The Bolivians improved week by week. I still remember the first Saturday when their team defeated our team. It was an amazing moment. Our teams were equally matched.

I would miss this routine when we returned to Canada. I often wondered how Jaimie was doing and how the "league" was going, but I heard no news. Many years later, we received a note from Jaimie. He told us the league had expanded in Cochabamba and then formed in La Paz and

Santa Cruz. It was now a national league with teams playing against each other. They had some sponsors and now had good equipment, umpires, and uniforms. Indeed, he indicated that the "championship finals" had been televised on national TV, and that his team had won the national championship. He was exuberant and thanked us for playing against them. This had sparked a whole new sport for Bolivia.

So what did we learn from the fastball encounters? It was an excellent opportunity to interact with Bolivians and form long-term friendships. It united the missionary community — which was badly needed. Doctrinal differences were set aside in a common pursuit of relaxation, friendship, and enjoyment. It developed into a national league which, I understand, is going to this day. Sometimes I jokingly say that helping to create that fastball league is likely the most important thing I ever did in Bolivia. Maybe it's not a joke. Maybe it's true. Maybe this was another example of God's sense of humour. It is one more opportunity for us to laugh along with God.

The Death of My Father and the Miracle of Mail

My mother died on July 30, 1963, when I was eighteen years old and just a few weeks after I graduated from high school. It was also the same time that I left home to go to teacher's college. I was the youngest of eight siblings and the last to leave home, which meant Dad was now by himself. He stayed on the farm for a few more years but moved into a basement apartment in Winkler for the winter months. Then he sold the farm and bought a modest home in Winkler.

My father enjoyed fishing.

He lived alone for the next eight years. We began to hear some rumours of a lady friend that was coming into his life. On September 4, 1971, he married Susan Janzen, a wonderful companion to him, a good mother to us, and an amazing grandmother to our children. She brought joy into my dad's life again, and they enjoyed their married life. We were very fortunate that she became such an integral part of our family unit.

As we were preparing to leave for Bolivia in 1980, we visited Mom and Dad for the last time. They were healthy and happy. They were excited about our new adventure, although Dad, always the cautious person, wondered about our capacity to live in a culture we didn't know. "Dad," I said, "we can only know it by living in it." They gave us their sincerest blessing to go.

There was a tinge of sadness in my father, and we wondered what that was about. At one point he said: "I won't see you again." It was a stark statement, with no "maybe" or "perhaps." We reassured him that this was not the case. Our assignment was only five years, he was in good health, and only seventy-six years of age. There was no reason to believe he would not see us again. We said our goodbyes, and his tears brought out our tears.

Communication was more difficult in those days. Phone rates for international calls were exorbitant; email, Facebook, and electronic mail did not exist. The Mission Board did not have any policies for home leave before the five year commitment was finished, so the only regular communication outlet we had was the postal service: letters and the occasional parcel.

We quickly discovered, however, that the mail service to Bolivia was very slow. We would write letters regularly and receive letters from my father, but we needed to count on a minimum of four weeks for the letters to arrive. To my knowledge, we never got correspondence from Canada in less that three to four weeks; often it could be five to eight weeks.

We kept in close touch with my father. Their life was good and full. His second marriage was a blessing to them both. We were glad.

My father with his new bride, Susan Janzen, 1971.

On Friday, March 23, 1984, I had finished another hectic week of teaching at the seminary. At our lunch table, we had remembered that this was my oldest sister's birthday, and we hoped that the birthday card we had sent would have arrived by now. Later, our phone rang, and it was a long-distance call from Canada. Very unusual. It was my brother. He informed us that our father had died that day. He and Susie had been having lunch. She got up to get something from the stove, and when she returned, my father was slumped over in his chair, dead. It was a huge shock to her — and to us. He died of congestive heart failure.

We cried. We had been looking forward to seeing him in just over a year. His prediction that he would not see us again had come true. We made immediate plans to go home for the funeral.

The next day, I went downtown Cochabamba to our travel agent's office. Thankfully, she was able to get airline tickets for all five of us to leave on Monday. The funeral had been scheduled for Wednesday. While I was downtown, I also dropped in at the post office to pick up mail. There was a letter from my dad. It had been written on Monday of that week, and was stamped on Tuesday. It had arrived in our mailbox in four days — an absolute miracle. We had never received a letter that quickly.

We opened the letter, and Dad's premonition about an impending death was clear in his writing. It was kind of a farewell letter — not totally overt, but clear enough. It was more than his usual cautious, pessimistic self. It was a letter of goodbye. In it he expressed his love for us and how proud he was that we were doing what we were doing. He also indicated that he was well, but that another year was a long time. He missed us.

In the face of this sudden phone call, what a gift it was to receive this miracle letter. We have no explanation for the speed with which it got there. It had never happened before, and it never happened again.

It was very good to go home to Winkler for the funeral. I remember that I stood alone by his coffin in the funeral home for a long time. I was overcome by emotion. I realized that not only had my father died, there was now no living generational buffer between me and my past. I was now that buffer for my children. It was sobering. My dad had been a quiet and reliable pillar in my life. Now he was gone. I was grateful again for the family that nurtured me.

Close Encounter with Liberation Theology: Old Stories Come to Life

Living and teaching in Latin America for ten years brought us face to face with Latin American Liberation Theology. It has been an enriching journey. I won't go into a long, detailed discussion here, but I would be amiss if I didn't mention it. It has had a profound impact on me, on my reading of Scripture, and on the ways in which I interpret the Christian life.

Jack engaging a group of pastors and leaders in Ethiopia, 2007.

Liberation Theology emerged out of Latin America in the 1950s and '60s. It felt like a significant challenge to me, to my church, and to my tradition. Why? Basically it says that theology, Bible reading, and ethics are influenced not only by what we read, but by the context from which we read it. In other words, the social/political context of the reader will dramatically impact what we see in a text we are reading. For example, slaves will see the biblical story of the Exodus — the Hebrew people's escape from tyranny in Egypt — to mean that God wants people to be free and doesn't condone slavery. Slave owners may read the same story and interpret it in a symbolic way that means we are sinners and need to be saved from the sins that enslave us. Therefore we should treat our slaves better, so that we can be better Christians. The impact on ethics (how we behave) will be very different depending which reading we prefer.

Liberation Theologians point out that not only does context influence our reading, but that there is no such a thing as a non-contextual reading. There is no "neutral" or "objective" reading of Scripture. Their effort, then, is to read Scripture from the perspective of the poor, the marginalized, the persecuted, the oppressed. And, lo and behold, when we do that we see things differently. For example, affluent people (Europeans and North Americans, they say) will read the story of the Good Samaritan in the New Testament, and immediately applaud the Samaritan for helping the person who had been injured by the thieves, and understand that we should do that too. This is a reading from the perspective of privilege. Another way to read this story is from the perspective of the victim and the thieves. Why was it necessary for thieves to look for money or resources? What was it about their lives that made thieving necessary? And why do social/political systems generate categories of people who are outsiders, like the Samaritan?

In their re-reading process, the Liberation Theologians try to demonstrate that Scripture reveals that God has a "preferential option for the poor," and that we should live our lives in the same way. What does that mean for middle-class Christians, such as me, or rich Christians?

They also indicate that in the history of the church, the "northern" church has increasingly shifted the central biblical message from liberation via obedience, to salvation via belief. This means that doctrine has replaced ethics and lifestyle as the primary measurement of salvation. It also means that salvation has been internalized and personalized, whereas the biblical perspective is that liberation is also social, political, and communal. Salvation is not only personal, it is also systemic. These are significant challenges to what I had learned in Winkler, Winnipeg, and Elkhart.

Should this really be a threat or a challenge? As I got more informed about this theological movement, I noticed that frequently they drew on Anabaptist perspectives to explain their understanding. They were inspired by my own theological roots, whereas I felt significantly challenged by their perspectives. What was going on? This process, then, forced me not only to understand their movement more profoundly, it challenged me to understand my own tradition more rigorously.

I noted, for example, that the Liberation Theology folks were drawn to Hans Denck's famous line: "You cannot truly know Christ unless you follow him in life" (Denck was an important Anabaptist leader in sixteenth century Germany). In this statement they find support for their perspective. "Knowing" Christ is not measured by believing doctrines about Christ, but by discipleship to him. They also pointed to Menno Simons' statement that: "True evangelical faith cannot lie sleeping. But it feeds the hungry, clothes the naked...." Again, this perspective shifts attention from doctrinal, or propositional belief, to following the example of Jesus in everyday life.

This perspective was brilliantly summarized by Dom Hélder Câmara, Catholic archbishop in Brazil, who stated: "When I helped the poor, they said I was a saint; when I asked: 'Why are they poor?' they said I was a communist."

I noted, however, that there were also some significant discrepancies between the conclusions they drew from what appeared to be common emphases with my own roots. The Liberation theologians, for example, expertly sketched the dire context in which Christians in Latin America live and discern obedience to Jesus. It has been a centuries-long context of oppression, poverty, and persecution against the poor people, often aided and abetted by the Christian church and Christian theology. This focus is indisputable. Indeed, it has been a context similar to the context of Jesus himself: a context of colonial empire (Rome), military occupation, daily oppression of the population (paying taxes to Caesar and forcible co-option by the occupying soldiers), and brutal suppression of critics (crucifixion). It seemed to me, however, that many (not all) of the theologians were then too willing to employ the same system of violence and brutality to make the needed changes toward peace, justice, and equality. Some openly advocated armed revolution as the only means to change the dire situation. Most did not question profoundly the embedded assumptions that certain dire contexts "justify" the use of violence to change it. This was, of course, a re-stating of the "just war" criteria first articulated by Saint Augustine in the fourth century AD. My reading of my own tradition and the experience of Jesus in Scripture was that precisely in this response is where Jesus is most innovative. While living in a similar context, his response was different. He taught that in situations such as this, we must not use the same toolbox of oppression that the oppressors were using. We needed to break the cycle of violence by our willingness to die for rather than to kill our enemies. We needed to "love our enemies" and "turn the other cheek."

There were some Liberation theologians who also recovered this part of the story of Jesus and the Anabaptist focus. But they were few. I felt a close kinship to those that included this aspect of Scriptural interpretation.

These challenging, and at times disturbing, insights by the Liberationists led to an exciting process of detective work. I needed to find clues in their movement, in my theological roots, and, most importantly, in my reading of Scripture and articulation of theology. This agenda was enough to keep me motivated and inspired. It still does.

So what have I discovered in this journey? First, I am grateful for this exposure and challenge. I have come to believe that I needed it, my tradition needs it, and the Christian church as a whole needs it badly. It is a tool for spiritual renewal. Second, it has highlighted for me the importance of exegeting (examining carefully) not only the Scriptural text, but also the context in which we read the text and the questions we bring to it. And thirdly, I have been amazed at the sustained relevance my Anabaptist roots have for contemporary faithfulness. And sometimes, we are the ones that are most blind to this potential. It takes others to see what we no longer see.

I think — or at least I hope — these challenges have left me more open to other adjustments needed in my understanding of faithfulness to God. Having three adult sons, all of whom are trained in biblical and theological understanding that goes well beyond my own, has persistently opened further insight to me. I am grateful and fortunate. I thank God for the ongoing excitement of discerning faithfulness, not only for myself but for the churches of my tradition.

Family music at our 25th wedding anniversary
celebration in Winkler, Manitoba, 1990

Cuba: Close Encounter with Fidel Castro

From 1985-89, we took a four-year hiatus from our Latin American assignment to finish my doctoral work in New Testament studies. I would do this at the Toronto School of Theology, and we decided to live in Kitchener.

My presence back on Canadian soil resulted in another life-changing opportunity. In 1986, I was invited by the Mennonite Central Committee to represent the Mennonite churches on an ecumenical visit by Canadian church leaders to Cuba. This delegation was sponsored by the Canadian Council of Churches, and our hosts would be the Cuban Council of Churches.

I was eager to go. My family and I had flown over the island of Cuba on our way in and out of Bolivia several times, and I had often commented on my desire to get to know the Cuban experiment under Fidel Castro more profoundly. Our experience in Latin America had convinced me that the systems as they had existed for at least 500 years had not worked well for the huge majority of Latin Americans. The so-called "trickle-down" theory of capitalist economics had failed. The wealth and potential of Latin American countries had not trickled down to benefit the masses of people. Rather, wealth had gushed out into the colonial empires: Spain, Portugal, France, Britain, and the United States of America. The trickle-down had resulted in the repetitive rape of Latin American resources at the expense of local populations and for the benefit of ruling classes of colonial powers and their puppets installed as authorities. Latin America was often described as the "underbelly" of First-world capitalism. The systems had worked well for the colonial powers; they had back-fired for the millions of people in Latin America.

In 1959, Castro installed an alternative vision in Cuba. It was designed to have Cuban wealth benefit the Cubans. He sought support for his alternative experiment. Unfortunately, he found it primarily with the Soviet Union. Slowly, the 1959 Cuban experiment became a communist experiment, although Castro himself had never joined the existing Communist Party in Cuba. His was more of a nationalist experiment using some communist tools, rather than an ideologically pure Marxist system.

This invitation would allow me to get to understand the Cuban experiment more profoundly.

I was the only Mennonite in this delegation of ten Canadian church leaders. I believe I was also the only one who was fluent in Spanish.

We landed in Varadero, Cuba, about a two-hour bus ride from Havana. There to meet us was the small, dynamic president of the Cuban Council of Churches. He was our host, and his name was Raul Suárez. He was a Baptist pastor and the founder-director of the Martin Luther King Junior Centre in Havana.

We got on the bus for our ride to Havana. He took the microphone, welcomed us all to Cuba, and then he said something surprising: "I understand there is a Mennonite among you. Can you please identify yourself and come up to the front. I want to sit with you on our trip into Havana." What a welcome. I identified myself and went and sat with him. For the next two hours, he outlined his very passionate convictions that the only theological current missing in Cuba was the one they needed the most, namely the Anabaptist current. He had "discovered" this theological option almost by accident, but he was intrigued and wanted to know more. He was convinced that his role was to help to "Anabaptize" Cuba. Little did I know that this initial conversation would result in well over fifty visits to Cuba (I've lost count), always working with Cuban church leadership (of all denominations) to teach and engage aspects of biblical, theological, and Anabaptist understandings of the Gospel. I am grateful to Raul for initiating me into these invigorating opportunities that we have had.

Jack and Irene with Rev. Raul Suárez: Cuban Baptist pastor and founding director of the Martin Luther King Centre in Havana, Cuba.

Another surprise awaited us that week. Half-way through the week, Raul informed us that Fidel Castro's office had called, and that he would be interested in a conversation with our delegation. He wondered if we would be interested. We, of course, were very interested. Fidel cleared his schedule and invited us to come to his office a few days later for an evening appointment. We had no agenda. Apparently, he was musing about the often rocky relationship his government had experienced with the churches in Cuba, and, it seemed, wanted to engage us on some things.

We went. His office was on the third floor of an inconspicuous building abutting the Plaza of the Revolution. The security was very light — just handing in our cameras to the aide. Fidel met us at the door of his office all decked out in his military fatigues. He was tall and warm. He shook each of our hands and gave us each a big Cuban cigar. His office was sparse, with basic furniture. Then, another surprise. Instead of the anticipated, formal, brief conversation of protocol, he invited us in for the "duration." We stayed for a lengthy conversation with very broad items of discussion. I will recount here only a few points that have been of most interest to me.

He was very relaxed and listened carefully. He had a young translator beside him, and she was excellent. It was apparent, however, that he understood English perfectly, and at some points interrupted her translation to insert a better word or phrase.

He asked what we had seen thus far. We responded that we had been to a women's prison, to a seniors' care home run by Catholic nuns, to a school for special needs children, to a community project for urban agriculture, to a cultural centre where the African traditions were being renewed, and so on. He asked if we had seen the efforts of the revolution for cultural development, literacy, free medical care for all, housing and employment for all, and so on. We said that we had been exposed to this as much as our short stay had permitted. He said: "I know you are all religious people. You must think about heaven a lot." We chuckled, and one delegate indicated that yes we do, but we also think about the condition and challenges of earth. In a somber and solemn tone, he asked: "From what you have seen so far, and the efforts of the revolution to help Cubans, do you think there might be room in heaven for me?" There was silence. He wasn't joking. We weren't sure how to respond. Finally, one member of our delegation responded: "We have been impressed by what has been accomplished. Thankfully, your question about room in heaven is not for us to answer. That will be God's decision, not ours. And God won't be asking our advice." Fidel laughed and went on to another topic.

He showed us a book he held in his hand. It was a new biography of Fidel, hot off the press that week, written by a Brazilian priest. Apparently, Fidel had spent some time with the author during the last six months or so and was interested in the result. He said he had just begun to read it, but had already noticed a significant mistake. He opened the book at

p. 19 and pointed. "This is wrong," he said. "Here it says that the Cuban revolution was inspired by Karl Marx and *The Communist Manifesto*. That is not true. It was inspired by a carpenter from Nazareth who went up a mountain to teach his people how to live."

He then shared a bit about his own experience with the church in Cuba — the Catholic Church. He grew up in a Catholic home and was sent to Jesuit schools. He learned about Jesus from the priests and developed quite an interest and curiosity about him. He reminded us that his experience was pre-Vatican II. [Vatican II was the effort by the Catholic Church to update itself in the early 1960s. Very significant changes came into the life of the church at that point.] He said he went to church, but the mass was entirely in Latin, and he could not understand anything. The Bible was read in Latin. He asked his parents to tell him more, and Bibles were not permitted in homes. And if they were, they were not permitted in Spanish. The Catholic Church was a large landowner at that time in Cuba. It controlled the educational system that was accessible only to a small percentage of the population. It opposed social/political change that could have improved conditions for the masses of people.

And then he made an interesting comment: "If the Catholic Church in Cuba in 1959 would have been like the Catholic Church in Nicaragua in 1980, there never would have been a Cuban Revolution as we know it. I would have dedicated my passion and vision for change through the Church." It was a sobering statement.

At another point, he talked about the issues of church and state in Cuba. His point was that the state wants to be non-discriminatory toward all faiths in Cuba, and for that reason, it was declared to be "atheist" in orientation. He did not mention this, but we were aware that Cuban Christians were not allowed to hold political office or participate in political processes. But, he continued, they were in the process of looking at this question and asked for our counsel.

I dared to speak up. I said (in Spanish) that their desire to be non-discriminatory was to be lauded. But that actually the state was, indeed, discriminating against Christians because public processes were not open to Christian participation. I indicated that "atheism" is as much a position of "faith" as Christianity. "To say that there is no God is a statement of faith," I said, "just as it is a statement of faith to say that there is a God." Therefore, I concluded, they were in fact discriminating on the basis of faith — one faith was allowed to participate, the other one was not.

He listened intently, looked at me, sat back in silence for a moment, stroked his beard (as he often did) and replied: "Thank you; I have never quite thought about this from that perspective."

Six years later, the Cuban constitution was changed in which the state was declared to be a "lay" state, not an "atheist" state. As a "lay" state, all citizens were allowed to participate in public processes because the state has "no religious opinion."

Sometimes in my less humble moments, I like to think that perhaps my comment was like a grain of sand on a public beach that contributed to this significant change. But then my humility quickly takes over, and I disregard this as fantasy.

The conversation with Fidel was very wide-ranging. He asked about the differences among evangelicals. He wanted to understand better why there were so many branches. He was very impressed that our delegation included a Catholic representative, a form of collaboration that neither Catholics nor Protestants would be willing to do in Cuba. He talked about agricultural issues, and expressed gratitude to Canada for significant help in the dairy industry. The interaction was real: he asked and he listened. We also asked. We asked him what he saw as the most significant challenge to the ongoing journey of the revolution. His response was immediate. He said that greatest challenge is to keep the revolution "green," that is, keep inspiring the younger generations with the aspirations of the revolution given that they had never experienced pre-revolutionary times. How similar, we thought, to the life of the church.

Finally, he asked if we had been to the Isle of Youth, a small island off the south coast of Cuba. The former dictator Fulgencio Batista had used this island for his prisons. Fidel himself had been held there for a time in one of the brutal prisons. After the revolution, they had closed all these prisons and transformed them into technical schools for international students. Many of the poorer countries, especially from Africa, were invited to send promising students there to receive free education in all sorts of trade and technical areas.

We indicated we had not been there and that it was not on our schedule. He insisted, and said: "Oh, you have to go there. It is important." And he indicated that he would make his own, private, military plane available to us for a visit that Saturday. And so we did. On Saturday, a van picked us up and drove us to a military airport west of Havana. There, his plane, pilot, crew, and personal advisor were awaiting us. We were flown to the island and spent the entire day touring the schools and visiting with students and teachers.

After more than two hours of conversation, Fidel wished us well and thanked us for the visit. We thanked him for his time. As we left, we noted that there was still another delegation that was waiting to see him. We were told that this kind of schedule was normal for him, as four hours of sleep per night was all he needed.

Presidential office building in Havana, Cuba.

It was a rare and remarkable opportunity. We were able to see Fidel in his unguarded moments. He was personable; he was a good listener; he did not dominate the conversation; he seemed to be genuinely interested in learning. All these characteristics were in stark contrast to his public image on TV and in articles and books about him. We also learned that he is human. He admitted to failures even as he was proud of achievements. We learned that he is a person of high aspirations and significant passion for his social vision. We learned that he has sacrificed his life to his social vision for Cuba.

Much later, as Fidel grew old and then sick, we watched his physical deterioration in sporadic appearances on TV. At one point he made his farewell speech, like a deathbed speech, to the Cuban congress. As I watched his deterioration and eventually his death (November 25, 2016), I could not help but feel a deep sense of sadness. My sadness was not so much generated by his death. It came, rather, from a profound sense that the Church had failed him. He was in a process of searching and tried to find answers in the Church from the priests. He discovered a Church whose primary message was inaccessible to him, and that was abetting the injustices in Cuban society. And so he turned to other avenues for change. There is no doubt that Fidel has much blood on his hands. But the idea that the use of violence is justified when the context calls for it is also something he learned from the Church. Ever since the fourth century AD, the Church has taught that violence can be justified when circumstances dictate it. In this sense, his efforts were not different than the French Revolution, the American Revolution, the American Civil War, World War I and II, and countless other efforts to make things better through violence.

His question is still with me: Do you think there might be room for me in heaven? I am aware that his spiritual search continued right to the end, and I hope I get to meet him again in heaven.

Colombia: The Rubber Hits the Road: How Much Sacrifice is Too Much?

We arrived in Bogotá, Colombia, for our new assignment with the church in mid-August, 1989. They had prepared a nice apartment for us on the third floor in a bustling section of the city. We were on Calle 63, and the church offices were on Calle 32. A thirty-one block walk to work along the busiest route in Bogotá. It was good. But then, two weeks after our arrival the bombs began.

Pablo Escobar, the popular head of a Colombian drug cartel, had made some noises about entering politics and running for the senate. The cartel had operated for decades, and Escobar was unimaginably rich. But threatening the political establishment — or oligarchy, as Colombians frequently referred to their system — was an unwelcome escalation of his power. The government began to focus on Escobar's drug business, and basically declared war on the cartel. Escobar, of course, did not sit idly by.

The drug war moved from the countryside into the urban centres — Bogotá being the one of those. It started small. Men or women with executive briefcases would go into a targeted office — a police station, government tax or other offices, banks, industries owned by key political figures — and "forget" the briefcase there. They were explosive devises that would kill, maim, and injure those who happened to be nearby. This was usually accompanied by a note that indicated those responsible and why this target was chosen.

Slowly, these bombs increased in size and strength. First, motorcycle bombs; then car bombs, and finally truck bombs. It just so happened that the zone we lived in was a particular target. There were any number of key offices and business establishments there that were of interest to the cartel. Our middle and youngest sons were with us. As the violence increased, our boys got to be experts in telling the difference between gun-shots, bombs, or firecrackers. We repeatedly heard all three from our apartment window. They also developed a good ear for guessing the distance the bombs were from our apartment. That one was four blocks away, that one was ten blocks, that one was two blocks. The intensity seemed to increase on weekends. We spent many a Friday evening guessing how close the bombs were to our place.

Most of the foreign-based businesses, mission boards, and other organizations pulled their employees out of Colombia. The ex-patriot community dwindled. The question arose whether we should consider leaving as well. Our mission bosses said that we should discern that with the local church leaders. We received a call from the Canadian Embassy encouraging us to leave. And if we didn't leave, at least to be as "inconspicuous" as possible. This, we joked, was quite impossible with one son well over six feet tall, and another one as blond as could be. Try being inconspicuous on the street with them around. The Colombian church leaders and others were very supportive of us. After some particularly close bombings, we would get phone calls assuring us of the prayers of the church. One day the leaders came for a visit. They indicated that the situation was getting quite serious and dangerous. They said that if we wished to leave, it was entirely understandable, and they would bless that. If we decided to stay, they would do everything in their power to support and accompany us. "This is not your problem to solve," they said. "It is fine for you to have an exit strategy. The church doesn't have one, but you can." The decision was ours.

We decided to wait and see a bit longer. The intensity of the war was not dropping. Our zone continued to be a special target. On our walk home from church on Sunday mornings, we would sometimes stop at a roasted chicken place for Sunday lunch. One Sunday we had our lunch and went home. About thirty minutes later, that chicken establishment was blown up. On another day, at about 7:30 am, our boys were off to catch their ride to school when there was an enormous blast. The windows in our apartment shook; some were broken. The boys quickly returned home, somewhat shaken. This one, they said, was very close. Likely within a block of our apartment. We huddled inside awaiting further news that was bound to come quickly due to the evident size of the blast. When word came, we discovered that the DAS building had been blown up. The DAS is the Colombian version of the FBI/CIA. They had an eight or so story office building. A large truck loaded with dynamite had parked in front of the building, and the truck bomb ignited. It was a huge blast. But, it was about seventy blocks for our apartment in quite another part of the city.

The possibility of leaving came up again and again. One day we were again discussing how to stay safe and inconspicuous. Obviously, the only way was to stay inside. I clearly remember our eighteen-year-old middle son, Derek, sitting on the couch. He looked at us with a determined look, and said: "Mom, Dad: I did not come to Bogotá to sit in an apartment." That was a significant turning point. We decided to stay and live as normal a life as we possibly could. We would be prudent, but not terrorized. We would be smart, but not panic. We did have very good role models for how to deal with this situation. We just needed to look at our Colombian brothers and sisters — our peers in the church. They had no "exit strategy." They were in this for the long haul. They lived their lives as normally as possible.

And so we stayed when not many of our North American compatriots did. We went about our assignments as normally as we could. The war continued without let-up for about eleven months, and then continued in waves of escalation and de-escalation. Escobar was found and killed on December 2, 1993 — four and a half years after our arrival. The urban violence began to lessen a bit.

During that whole time, we began to experience what our brothers and sisters were experiencing. Every Sunday we would go to church, and on most Sundays there were reports from church families of love ones killed, kidnapped, or disappeared. The church went on being the church. The Mennonite Biblical Seminary of Colombia was organized in the first five months of our work. The Latin American Anabaptists Resource Centre was organized in the first four months of our work. A year later, the church initiated a new venture called JustaPaz, a centre for Peace and Justice dedicated to confronting the horrendous violence in the country. Within a year, the church organized a program for Conscientious Objection to military service — a concept largely unheard of until they began their work. A year after that, in 1992, conscientious objection was embedded in the new Colombian constitution largely due to the efforts of the Mennonites. The church used their small farm an hour and a half outside of Bogotá as a safe haven for internally-displaced refugees fleeing the drug and revolutionary strife in the countryside. This time of intense violence was also a time of unprecedented courage and creativity in the church.

Jack teaching seminary class in Bogotá.

They did also experience extreme loss. The president of the Mennonite Church, who was also the Executive Director of World Vision Colombia, was gunned down on a visit to Lima, Peru. He was on his way to a meeting, and two men on a motorcycle passed him. The one in the back had a machine gun and riddled José with over forty bullets at close range. The church reeled at this tragedy. He had been a keen and alert leader. His administrative skills were exceptional. I remember the speaker at his funeral say that we mourn the death of José now, but it will take the church at least forty years to recover from his absence. That has proved to be true.

We were blessed to share five years with the church in Colombia. It became increasingly apparent to us that the most important thing we ever did in Colombia was simply to stay there. We weathered the storm with them. This generated a level of trust and credibility in our work that was crucial. We continue to thank God for safety in spite of our naivety. We thank the Colombian Church for supporting us, accompanying us, and inspiring us in understanding what it means to be the Church. And we thank our friends, family, and the Canadian/USA churches for supporting our ministry in Colombia. Some have criticized us for taking too great a risk. Maybe they are right. How much risk is too much? It was a life-changing experience. God is faithful.

Close Encounters with the FARC (Revolutionary Armed Forces of Colombia)

I mentioned above the war in Colombia between governmental forces and the Medellin Drug Cartel led by Pablo Escobar. This was not the only war going on. In addition to the conflict with the cartel, Colombia was involved in a fifty-year-old revolutionary struggle with several revolutionary (usually know as guerrilla) forces. The largest, best organized, and best armed of these was the FARC (Revolutionary Armed Forces of Colombia). There was also the EPN (The National Popular Army) and the EPL (The Popular Liberation Army). These armed groups began in the 1960s with some social/political agenda such as land distribution, social poverty, democratic equality, and many other items. These concerns were still there but were often not too visible in their struggle just to survive. They continued their guerrilla activities and tactics throughout these decades, sometime with more strength, sometimes with less.

During the years we lived in Colombia, the revolutionary forces were strong, especially the FARC. There were daily killings, kidnappings, disappearances, threats, and bombs. It was confusing to try to separate these wars against the revolutionary forces and the cartels. And most would agree that they could no longer be entirely separated. The primary source of funding for the revolutionary forces was their partnerships with the cartels. Adding to the confusion was the documented fact that the Colombian military and some politicians were also deeply enmeshed with the drug cartels and benefitted from the war.

It was a very difficult, violent, and insecure context. Sociologists called it a "culture of death." Colombia was the most violent country in the western hemisphere.

The Colombian Mennonite Church was heavily involved in being the church in this difficult context. Their organizations worked directly with the victims of war, with the refugees (internally displaced people), with the landless whose land had been taken away, with issues of family reunification, with documentation of lawless acts, and with conscientious objection to obligatory military service. This put them into the cross-hairs of the military and the revolutionary forces alike — all of who were recruiting increasingly younger members. They worked with legal issues arising due to the conflict, with sanctuary options for those targeted in the wars, and with attempts to build bridges of understanding among and between the warring parties. This meant that they were potentially friends and enemies of all the groups, including the governmental forces.

They were regularly named in the death lists that were published by the actors of war, indicating that they were targets of war. Our seminary office was invaded by a heavily armed group that took our computers for purposes of gleaning information. A group like the church that had access to military generals, FARC commanders, EPN camps, and government politicians raised suspicions and eyebrows. The Mennonites were respected, loved, and hated. They were seen as friend and foe in the same breath. Bridge-builders were both respected and misunderstood by all sides.

I, personally, have had three significant encounters with various parts of these armed groups. I will tell these stories in the sequence they happened.

Encounter 1:

In early 1998, Andrés Pastrana was elected as president of Colombia. He had run on a ticket promising new initiatives for peace. On November

7, 1998, he made a bold move. The FARC had taken over a very large part of southern Colombia — a 42,000 square km. tract about the size of Switzerland. It was centred around the small town of San Vicente del Caguán in the southern Andes. Pastrana knew that sending in the military would result in countless dead with no guarantee of success. He told the leadership of the FARC that the government would cede that land to them for three years and they would be given the authority to "govern" that tract of land for that period of time. The Colombian military would not enter, but there were conditions. The FARC needed to set up a "peace table" and guarantee security to anyone who wished to use it for the purposes of peace processes and creating peace proposals. The FARC was also prohibited from bringing in additional weapons during this time, and the Colombia military, with USA support, set up camps on the roads leading into this territory to enforce the ban on weapons. The FARC commanders accepted this offer with the conditions and took over the territory. They set up a literal "table" under a tree close to their headquarters in San Vicente. The table was dedicated for peace initiatives. There was a slight promise of hope in the air. Creative alternatives to peace between opposing partners could now be imagined in a situation where security was guaranteed — albeit by the FARC troops. Many thought it was a ploy on the part of the FARC commanders — a trap for assassination and kidnapping. Others felt that this initiative needed a chance to succeed.

There were many evangelical churches in this territory that was now under the control of the FARC commanders — although none of them were Mennonite. The pastors and leaders of the churches were theologically confused. In Romans 13, the Apostle Paul says that everyone should be "subject to governing authorities." Evangelicals wanted to honour that, but who were the "authorities" in the territory? Was it still Pastrana and his troops even though they could not enter? Was it now the FARC commanders who were beginning to demand things of them that they didn't like? Should their young people be recruited into FARC troops instead of into the Colombian military? Did they need to obey? What should they do? They needed help.

They knew of the Mennonites because of their broad bridge-building ministries. They phoned the Mennonite Church headquarters in Bogotá and asked if it would be possible to send someone for a four- to five-day workshop of Bible study, prayer, and reflection to help their pastors struggle with the complex questions they were facing. They indicated that this request had been approved by the FARC commanders, and security would be guaranteed. The Mennonite leaders said, yes, they would come. They arranged a date.

The Mennonite leaders suggested that because this territory was politically a "hot potato," it would be wise to send someone other than a Colombian, but one who knew the language, the political situation, and culture. They asked me if I would do this. I indicated I would under one condition: that some of the Colombians would accompany me. They agreed, and plans were made. They even gave me permission to bring along some interested folks from Winkler, which surely would be a mind-blowing experience for them.

We were to leave on a Friday afternoon and fly in a small chartered plane that could land on the runway in San Vicente. The workshop would begin that evening and go until the following Wednesday. They said they were expecting up to 125 pastors and leaders to attend.

The Thursday night national news — both printed papers, and television — carried a headline that "FARC Commanders Declare All Evangelical Pastors as Targets of War." It went on to explain that the FARC had evidence that evangelical pastors were often governmental spies feeding information to governmental sources. We, of course, were concerned. We would be gathering for five days with 125 evangelical pastors two blocks from the FARC headquarters in that region. We gathered, discussed, and prayed. The Colombian Mennonite leaders indicated in the end that they suspected the news article to be a hoax. After all, they said, "Truth is always the first victim of war." They said they continued to be willing to go, and I indicated the same based on their assessment. I asked the Winkler folks if they would rather stay back due to the heightened potential of risk. We decided to go before we left Winkler; this does not change our mind, they said.

So the next day we flew out on a small plane and landed on the airstrip in San Vicente. The FARC commanders, with their Jeeps and armed guard, met us as the bottom of the exit stairs of the plane. They smiled, warmly welcomed us to San Vicente, and gave us all hugs. They escorted us to a small hotel where we would be staying.

Encounter with two FARC commanders (unidentified) in San Vicente de Caguán, 1998. I was accompanied by Colombian leaders and some friends from Winkler, Manitoba (left to right): Dwight Suderman, Ike Friesen, David Hoeppner, Karl Enns.

I won't say more about the workshop itself, but there were a reduced number of pastors (seventy-five) and the workshop continued as planned. We had an excellent five days. Our Mennonite leaders asked for an audience with the commanders for Monday afternoon, and it was granted. Again, they received us warmly, and we sat down for a two-hour conversation with them. They offered us tea. We conversed about the workshop and the situation in the territory. They gave us an update about how many groups had so far taken advantage of the "peace table." They seemed pleased. Someone from our group asked about the Thursday night headline about Evangelical pastors being a target of war. They scoffed at this idea. They said that the state-governed media had likely heard about this initiative in San Vicente and were trying to derail it.

Walking to the church in San Vicente (left to right): Jack, David Hoeppner, Ricardo Esquivia, Dwight Suderman.

On my way out of the headquarters, one of the commanders was sitting at his desk by his computer. I noticed a whole stack of *VeggieTales* videos on the desk beside the computer. *VeggieTales* was a very popular effort to tell Bible stories and teach Christian values to children and adults alike. I asked him about the videos. He responded, and said, yes, his children really like them, and they play them all the time.

This was a reminder that FARC commanders are also human beings. They have spouses, children, and homes. They are committed to something important to them that is difficult for us to understand. They want to live, and they want to live well.

Encounter 2:

After decades of civil violence in Colombia, a summit for peace was organized by a broad range of actors, including the government, military, armed revolutionary groups, civil society, and both evangelical and Catholic churches. The hope was to get a broad spectrum of concerned groups together to analyze the present context in Colombia and to find ways toward peace. This summit was held on San Andres Island on February 13-17, 2006. Of course, the location was strategic. Where would groups in conflict with each other feel safe enough to send representatives? Security was a big issue. San Andres is a very small Colombian island off the coast of Nicaragua. It would be easier to secure the island and guarantee security for all.

My colleague and I from Mennonite Church Canada were specially invited to be an international presence at this summit. We accepted.

The evangelical churches were determined to come out of this summit with a joint statement of co-operation in efforts for peace. I was given a specific assignment: could I present a basic biblical/theological framework that would be helpful for them to think through these difficult issues of violence, justice, and peace? I prepared that, and it was well-received.

So we went. About 120 persons from a wide range of interested groups were there. The first two days were spent listening to contextual analyses from the various sectors of society. The data was grim. Violence seemed to be advancing unabated. There were attempts to find fault: why is this happening? Again, each group had its own analysis.

Then they began to think of potential solutions. It was at this point that something remarkable happened — at least from my perspective. Every time a solution was suggested, there was a realization that not all groups had free access to all nooks and crannies of Colombian territories. Some areas were controlled by the Colombian military where the revolutionary groups would not go. Other areas were controlled by revolutionary groups where government forces and politicians would not go. Yet, the solutions suggested required access to everyone, everywhere. Anything else seemed like stop-gap measures. And then a light went on: the only organization represented in that room that was present with the people in every part of Colombia was the Church — it was present in every nook and cranny of the national territory.

Then another light went on: what if the *Church* — each congregation — was an agent of peace, like a peace centre? Aha! There is the answer. It was bizarre. Here were all these politicians, military men, guerrilla leaders, business leaders — all in one voice — asking the Church to be centres of peace. It was like asking the Church to be the Church.

I couldn't help but smile. It was strange. And then they went into strategy sessions about how they could help the Church to be the Church. Perhaps if the pastors were better trained; maybe if the Sunday school material had a focus on peace; perhaps if sermons could teach about peace; ….maybe….perhaps…maybe. I believe it was quite a moment for the delegates from the churches that were present. Maybe this is what God had in mind all along. Maybe the Church should be a social reconciliation presence. Maybe the Church could generate a message and strategy of peace. It was quite remarkable.

In a nutshell, what happened is that folks came together to see how the political structures could function better for the peace of Colombia. Everyone agreed that if the Church had been, was, or would be the Church, it would be a powerful force forward toward this goal.

The churches worked together to produce a joint document. In it, they promised they would take steps to be the kind of peace churches that they should have been all along. The Church had learned a lesson. Now it remained to be seen if these would simply be empty words. On a visit to Colombia twelve years later, we were surprised that some of the Mennonite leaders were still using the theological framework that I had prepared for that encounter.

If the Church would be the Church — what a novel idea. I wondered if God was smiling — maybe even laughing at us. I wondered if we would welcome that smile and smile back.

Encounter 3:

Our third encounter with the FARC came in September 2018. We had been asked by a local tour agency to lead a learning tour to Colombia. We were eleven eager participants learning from the Colombian Church.

On the agenda on Friday, September 28, 2018, was an afternoon conversation with two high-ranking leaders of the FARC. The meeting would take place at the Mennonite Centre in central Bogotá. Our group members were both anxious and anticipating the conversation. They had never experienced this before. I encouraged them to think of their role in two ways: one, to be good, active listeners; two, to ask good questions. Some doubted their capacity to ask "good" questions. I assured them that it would be fine because these leaders are also simply humans.

But first a little background to the conversation.

Juan Manuel Santos was elected president in Colombia in 2010. He ran on a platform of negotiating a peace settlement with the FARC after almost sixty years of conflict. The FARC was also ready for a serious attempt to negotiate peace. The context was such that an effort to negotiate was possible.

President Raul Castro of Cuba offered to host the meetings in Havana, and to provide a safe-space in Havana where the dialogues could take place. Both the Colombian government and the FARC leadership accepted this invitation. They trusted Castro, and both sides could feel safe in Havana.

So, the negotiations began in 2012. Obviously, it was tough going. There was much on the agenda to be considered: reparation for the thousands of victims of the war; repatriation of land taken from peasant-farmers; justice and punishment for the perpetrators (both the FARC and the

Colombian military); truth-telling and unveiling the decades of lies and propaganda; the return of thousands of persons kidnapped during the conflict; the laying down of arms; the reincorporation of active combatants into civil society, family, and communities; the ongoing participation of the FARC in the political structure in Colombia; and much more. It was a daunting task, but both sides were committed to make it work.

The two sides managed to come to an agreement. The peace accords were signed by both parties on August 24, 2016, amid much celebration. But the deal needed to be ratified in a public referendum by Colombians. Many Colombians, meanwhile, had grown weary of the extended conversations and were not happy with some of the items in the peace accords. The referendum was held on October 2, 2016, and the proposed accords were defeated by a very slim margin: 49.8% in favour, 50.2% against. This was disappointing. Government and FARC negotiators went back to the table and renegotiated a few of the key points of most disagreement. The newly negotiated accords were taken back to the Colombian congress and ratified by both houses on November 29-30, 2016. "Peace" had come to Colombia, or had it? President Santos was awarded the Nobel Peace Prize for 2016. But the accords now needed to be implemented, which would not be simple.

One of the agreements in the accords was that the FARC would shift from being an armed, revolutionary army, to participating in the democratic process in Colombia via the formation of a new political party. Under the banner of the new party, they could run candidates in municipal and national elections. Another part of accords was that the FARC would be guaranteed a minimum of two senators and some representation in the house as well.

The two men we met in 2018 were high-ranking advisors to the senators then sitting in the senate. In other words, they were higher-ranking than the senators themselves. We were amazed that they would take time on a Friday afternoon to come to the Mennonite Centre for a conversation with eleven "nobodies" from Canada and the USA. But there we were.

Our meeting was led by two young men from the Colombian Mennonite Church. Both had much experience representing the Church in various pieces of the Church's peace initiatives. They had met the FARC leaders in other settings and were comfortable with each other. We all introduced ourselves, and the Mennonite leaders began with a prayer, and a brief explanation that we were there not simply because of Colombian politics, but because we were followers of Jesus of Nazareth who taught us to seek peace in non-violent ways. Symbolically, they placed an open Bible on the table and read a portion from the Sermon on the Mount. The FARC leaders seemed to be entirely comfortable with the prayer and the Christian framework that was presented. I needed to translate the entire conversation, both into Spanish and back into English.

The FARC leaders each gave a brief overview: one spoke of the history of the FARC; the other outlined the process of the peace negotiations and the key points in the peace accords. Both had been active members on the front lines of the FARC, and it was obvious that both had a significant amount of blood on their hands. They had joined the front lines as teenagers and had handed over their weapons only a little while previous due to the implementation of the peace accords. One of the young men was the son of the second-in-command of the FARC, a man well known for leading and participating in many of the massacres perpetrated by the FARC. His father had been killed in a bombing raid by the Colombian military.

It was clear that both wanted to start a new page. They spoke respectfully of past FARC leadership, but both insisted that now was the moment to take a new direction. They then detailed how the implementation of the accords was progressing two years after their approval, and the story was not encouraging. President Santos had lost the election in May 2018 to the Conservative Party, and the new president had not been in favour of the peace negotiations in the first place. The newly elected government was dragging their feet in the implementation of the process or ignoring it altogether. They indicated that the FARC had kept 100% of its word so far and was calling on the government to do the same.

They also indicated that their members could possibly lose patience with the non-implementation on the governmental side and pressure to go back to the mountains and into active resistance. They hoped it would not get that far.

Our tour members listened well and asked excellent questions. It became a frank, personal, emotional exchange on both sides. Finally, we stood in a circle, held hands, and the Mennonite leader led us in an amazing prayer. The FARC leaders seemed to be in no rush to leave. They felt good in the company of the group. There were many hugs and tears from both sides as we said farewell to these young men. It was an unforgettable experience.

Later in the comfort of our hotel, we debriefed with the learning group. How did you feel? How do you feel now? I asked them pointedly: how do you feel about hugging and holding the bloody hands of the FARC? One person responded: we don't need to make peace with friends, but it is precisely with the enemy that peace must be made. Another one said: if the early church could accept Paul to become an apostle, we can accept FARC members who have changed their minds. Another said: they are human beings like we are. They want the best for their families and children. Yet another said: I don't need to agree with a person in order to hug him and cry for him. I was moved by their stories.

Our learning group had an experience of a lifetime. They wanted to respond tangibly to efforts for peace that they had experienced in the Colombian Mennonite Church. In less than a month, they raised $25,000 among themselves to support JustaPaz, the Peace Centre of the Colombian Mennonite Church. The peace process continues. We continue to be called by Jesus to be ambassadors of peace. We are grateful to God and to the learning tour members for opening themselves to this experience.

The Art of Changing Structures in the Church: Integrating? Creating?

I began working at the head offices of Mennonite Church Canada in 1996. At that time, it was still called Conference of Mennonites in Canada. In case you're wondering (and you likely are not) this shift in names did not come easily. But it's a story worth knowing.

My first role was as the executive secretary of the Resources Commission (1996-99). This was the denominational department working with Christian Education and all the derivatives thereof. We worked with Sunday school materials, pastoral training, hymn book selection, publishing, schools at all levels, camps, and much more. It was challenging, and I had a great team to work with — both in the office and beyond.

Then the structural discussions began. It's complicated, but here's a synopsis. The Mennonite world in North America was divided into many different denominations, including the Old Order, Old Colony, Sommerfelder, Chortizer, Evangelical Mennonite, Evangelical Mennonite Mission Church, Mennonite Brethren, Mennonite Church, Conference of Mennonites in Canada — to name a few. The two largest of these were the Mennonite Church (Swiss Mennonite origins) and the General Conference Mennonite Church (Russian Mennonite origins). Our Canadian denomination was a part of the General Conference Mennonite Church.

Most of these denominations, including ours, were organized by continent: North America. That meant that both USA and Canadian churches were joined together under one denominational body. In Canada we were fortunate to have a Canada-wide body as well, but this was not the case in the USA. We had come through some very tough times — especially in the USA. There was the civil rights movement entwined with the extended war in Vietnam. The USA churches brought their considerable agenda to the North American body. The Canadian church brought it's immediate concerns to the Canadian body. This meant that more often than not, when Canadians went to the North America-wide committees or gatherings, the agenda was dominated by the USA national agenda. This increasingly became a problem. The Canadian agenda got very little attention in the North America-wide body.

The other issue was that more and more local congregations were becoming "dual" congregations. Some wanted to be members of one denomination, others of the other. The local solution was to become members of both. But that had its problems too. Local congregations were not able to carry the financial responsibility of both, much less be adequately represented in them.

In the 1990s, these denominations decided to take a careful look at their structures. At first, I was not too involved in these discussions. They were going on above my head and beyond my department. But little by little the fog began to lift, and it was clear that we were moving toward a merging of structures. Why have two major bodies when the belief systems were so similar that there was little noticeable difference? In about 1998 the word "integration" became the key word. Work was moving ahead to "integrate" the Mennonite Church with the General Conference Mennonite Church at a North American level.

One of the key departments that would need to be "integrated" was the department of Mission. Each denomination had its own Mission Board, and the Canadian church had its own as well. In addition, there were several regional Mission Boards in the USA. How could mission efforts be integrated? In each case, these boards handled the largest budgets of any denominational departments. In other words, the plan to integrate would be complex.

In 1999, the Canadian Conference asked if they could shift me out of the Resources Commission to head up the process of Mission integration on its behalf. I accepted the new assignment.

All levels of the denominational integration conversations and planning were moving full speed ahead. The Mission integration team included four partners from the USA and myself as the only Canadian. We worked hard. At times I was on the plane to the USA at least three to four times a month. Sometimes they all came to Canada to meet. We consulted very broadly. These were the days before Skype and Zoom. Face-to-face conversation was very important. The agenda was sensitive and explosive. But we worked well. It was challenging and enjoyable.

Then the winds began to shift. Yes, we continued to talk about "integrating" the two denominations, but in addition to integrating them it seemed wise to separate the integrated denominations along national borders. If that sounds confusing now, imagine how it sounded then. But the data and experience were undeniable. Yes, we all wanted the two churches to join into one. But, increasingly, we were convinced that the USA required its own nationwide church to deal with its nationwide agenda, and so did the Canadians. This seemed to complicate matters but, in my opinion, actually simplified things. I could now think of a Mission Board that would respond to the Canadian context and to Canadian interests. And so could my USA peers. We worked with two organizational consultants, both Lutherans, who were very helpful.

But there was still the question: just because the denominational structures decide to separate into national lines, do the Mission structures necessarily need to follow that as well? Most folks said we could still have one Mission Board for both countries. I became increasingly convinced that this would not work well. It would be better to divide the Mission structure into national lines as well. This was sensitive agenda. There had been centuries of strong loyalties built between the predominant Swiss background Canadian churches with Elkhart, Indiana, and the predominant Russian background Canadian churches with Newton, Kansas. These are the headquarters where "mission money" and mission loyalty were embedded. It would be difficult to shift that loyalty to Winnipeg. I argued that this same thing was true for the denominational structures themselves. There would need to be a "retraining" of loyalties at every level, so why not include the Mission Department in that.

I still remember clearly, after dozens of meetings trying to imagine the best Mission structures, our consultants asked all five of us to go off by ourselves. Our assignment was to summarize our months of discussions into a workable and preferred structural model. We would come back and share our models to determine what the next steps should be.

Off we went; each into our own corner. I designed a model based on separation: one agency for the USA and one for Canada, but cooperating in a whole variety of ways and designing strong partnership criteria. My point was that we are better partners to each other, and we can cooperate better if we are structural peers rather than to be structurally integrated. The continental structural models, I argued, would inevitably put Canadians into a minority position again, and the USA agenda would continue to dominate the structures.

After about an hour, we were called back. Each of us was asked to sketch our model on a blackboard. The outcome was, in a sense, riding on whether some consensus could be detected in the proposed models. The consultants suggested that the USA folks go first, and that I should go last. Strange suggestion, but I did not argue.

We sat back and saw the models emerge. All four before me came back with slightly nuanced integrated models. My heart began to sink. When my turn came, I did my best to acknowledge what had gone before, but that my model would be different. I sketched my model based on separation and articulated the rationale. It seemed to me that we were miles apart. I sat down feeling somewhat discouraged for being a fish out of water. The consultants asked us to remain in silence and contemplate the models before us. I don't think any of us saw a solution on the blackboard. After about five minutes of silence, one the consultants got up and I don't think I'll ever forget his words: "Ladies and gentlemen, I think we've got a model." We were all surprised. He was seeing something none of us were seeing.

He began to sketch all the areas of consensus in these models. We were in agreement on Purpose, objectives, mission, missiology, funding, personnel issues. Then he reminded us that we were using a "missional church" framework for our planning, a framework we were all enthusiastic about. He noted, however, that none of us had overtly applied that framework to the model we had sketched. He was right, although I had very much used it as a mental screen as I worked at the model.

So, we took another hour, and he led us meticulously through the foundational values and assumptions of the missional framework. With each point he asked us to consider the structural implications of what we were all equally affirming. When we completed that exercise, he asked us again to spend some time alone. When we came back together, there was unanimous agreement that the "separated" model would fit best with the missional framework. We did indeed have a model, and there was complete consensus in the group. It was amazing. Together we then fine-tuned that model and presented it to those overseeing the integration process.

Not only did we have a model, but in many ways our model became a model for other departments that were working. The end result was that the two large denominations indeed integrated but then decided to organize along national contexts. In 2001, this was approved by the General Conference Mennonite Church and one year later by the Mennonite Church. Mennonite Church Canada and Mennonite Church USA were born.

Was the Mission model a good decision? With twenty years of retro-vision, it is difficult to answer. The sad fact is that the Canadian mission structure has suffered significant demise, and the one in the USA is flourishing. So all things being equal, we could say that it was good for the USA but not good for Canada. But not all things have been equal. There have been too many additional factors not directly related to the model that have impacted the journey of each one. We are no longer comparing apples with apples or oranges with oranges. I continue to believe it was, and is, the best model for each. Mennonite Church USA has addressed its national context in ways it has never done before. It has addressed international partnerships by taking full ownership of its national context in the USA in ways that never were possible before. These shifts are welcome and were long overdue.

And Mennonite Church Canada? I think we just don't know. There are too many "what ifs" that are unrelated to the model, but which did impact it dramatically. We did what we could in the context we were living. We know that decisions always carry unanticipated consequences — collateral damage or friendly fire. That goes both ways. The Canadian mission model has also been impacted in unanticipated ways by concurrent decisions that were not directly related to it. At the time, with the pieces we had on the table, I do believe it was the best decision.

I remember that during this process of discussion and design, I was invited to speak at an assembly in Ontario. I carefully outlined the model we were proposing and the rationale for it. At one point, I made the statement: "Friends, the best is yet to come." There was resounding applause. I believe the rationale resonated well with this part of the constituency. I, for one, am still waiting for the "best yet to come."

Face to Face with Mennonite Church Canada

In 2005, I was invited to be the general secretary of Mennonite Church Canada. In some ways it made sense. I had worked as executive in the two largest departments: Mission and Education. After our return from Colombia in 1994, Irene and I spent two full years travelling full-time to churches all over North America reporting on our experiences. That gave us a good feel for the spirit and challenges of the churches.

On the other hand, I was not eager to accept this position at first. I was happy in what I was doing. I had excellent staff and an interesting and challenging ministry. There was no reason to take the next step. Yet, more and more people were tapping my shoulder. I remember we were talking to our oldest son about this in the summer of 2005. I laid out the pros and cons, and indicated the various levels of the church that were requesting me to make this move. I was still hesitant. At one point our son said, very forcefully: "What more do you need? You have taught us about the discernment of the Body, and the Body has discerned. So why aren't you listening?" That comment brought me up short. I think it was the turning point and allowed me to accept the invitation.

Shortly after that conversation, Irene and I were back in Rosthern, Saskatchewan, where we had lived for five years. We were just walking the streets and reminiscing about our years there, and we began to think about the next stage.

I asked myself — and her — the question: "What do I need most to do this next job well?" The answer came immediately. I needed to know anew and first hand the spirit, pulse, concerns, challenges, and needs of the 230 or so congregations that made up MC Canada. I felt deeply that to lead well, I needed to be in touch with the pulse of what was going on in the congregations. The congregations are spread over an immense territory all the way from Petitcodiac, New Brunswick to Vancouver Island; from the southernmost part of Canada in Leamington, Ontario, to the northern Indigenous communities in Manitoba. I knew that they were not only geographically distant, they were also diverse in every imaginable way: theologically, socially, economically, linguistically, and culturally. Then came the next question: "How would I best be able to feel the pulse?" This time the answer did not come easily. We began to brainstorm various options: go to the area church assemblies; do a survey of pastors; initiate online connections of some kind; create a plan to visit fifty congregations per year for the next five years. None of these options excited me very much. At some point in the conversation Irene made a very simple suggestion: "Visit them." I smiled and thought that it was a nice but impractical idea.

But that idea kept coming back and kept growing on me. Would it be possible to visit each congregation, in person, at their accustomed place of worship? I knew the geographical logistics would be daunting, but would it be possible?

I began my new position on December 1, 2005. It was no big deal because I simply moved my office over a few doors. The moderator of MC Canada came out for the day. We had a special morning coffee break with staff, and that was it. My new tasks were now on my table. Thankfully, we had been able to shift existing staff around to take over my previous duties. It felt like a seamless transfer of responsibilities.

I kept mulling the idea of visits to the congregations, but I didn't share it with my staff till the New Year. But if I was serous about this, it would be good to do early in my term and not drag it out. In early January 2006, the executive staff met to continue the strategic planning that had begun. I mentioned the idea of visits, and it immediately caught on. I was surprised. I then asked two of our staff members to work on a logistical plan to see if this would be possible. I didn't want to drag it over several years. I wanted to set aside a focused time to do it soon and quickly. I gave them the framework: it needed to be 100% of the 233 congregations, each one in their own place of worship. I did not want to meet them in groups or clusters; I did not want to meet congregational delegates in some restaurant in a nearby town to facilitate the logistics. I wanted to meet them at their place where they are enmeshed in their ministry. It was a tough assignment.

Within a week, they came back with a plan. It would cover 80% of the congregations with the conditions I had set, but for about 20% it would not be "realistic." They had done good work, but I sent it back with the instructions that it needed to be 100%. They came back with a 92% plan, and I indicated that it was not good enough. After several more days, they came back with a 100% plan, and it was a go. We began to plan for the visits.

We drew up some parameters for the visits: I would always be accompanied by at least one other executive staff member and at least one leader from the area church that we were visiting. We would spend ninety minutes with each congregation, and we would need to be very strict about the schedule. We would visit each one at their primary location of worship. We would not visit on Sundays, and we would not accept speaking engagements. We would not accept lunch or supper invitations from the congregations with the exception of some of the most remote locations. We would stay in hotels and not be billeted in homes because it would be a draining schedule. And it would be primarily a listening tour. Of the ninety minutes, our team would take nine minutes and the representatives of the congregations would share the other eighty-one minutes during which time we could ask questions for clarification and deepening the conversation. I would prepare a list of questions and ask them to respond to those questions during our ninety minutes. We would not dictate to them who would respond to us: they could decide that. It might be the board of deacons, the elders, the church council, the pastor(s), a Sunday school class, or young people.

They could decide who would be at the meeting and who would prepare the responses. We would be listening not only to the words but to their internal processes of preparing for our visits.

I decided that the questions would need to be very simple, yet allow us to enter deeply into sharing about the experience of the congregation. I came up with four simple yet substantive questions for the congregations: How are you? What are you doing? What are your concerns? What are your needs?

The logistical plan called for seventy-one days of visits. Most would take place in March, April, and May 2006, plus we would need a few weeks in October 2006 to finish all the visits. In areas where churches were clustered close together, we planned up to six conversations per day. In other areas, of course, it was fewer.

The experience of the visits was simply amazing. The idea "caught" or went "viral" in the congregations. We were warmly received everywhere, even in congregations that were not strong fans of MC Canada. The hospitality was exceptional. We drank more coffee and ate more cinnamon buns and doughnuts than ever before. Just because we had asked not to be invited for meals, didn't mean they didn't want to do something special. In many places, we would walk in on a weekday afternoon and there were 150 people there to meet us. There were farmers in overalls who stopped their tractors to come and participate. There were young mothers who changed their work shifts to make sure they could be there. There were young and old alike. Not everywhere, of course. In some places we were simply met by a group of deacons or the church council. But everywhere they had taken the four questions seriously and had worked diligently to respond. They were eager to share their story and their experiences.

The meeting format was simple. The executive staff person usually took a minute or two to thank them for having us and to explain again why we were there. Then we turned over the time to them. We would interrupt with questions here and there, which made the reporting dynamic and lively. At the end, I would take a few minutes to thank them, to remind who we are as a Church, and to emphasize the importance of the Body and their part in it. We prayed to finish the meeting.

Then came the most difficult part: we needed to get out to the car so that we would be on time for our next appointment — sometimes only fifteen minutes apart — but folks wanted to chat and talk more and ask questions. But they understood, and most of the time we managed to maintain our schedule.

We had carefully articulated the "objectives" of these visits in our pre-planning, but we underestimated what might happen in each point. In a least one point we missed out altogether. The biggest surprise — unexpected and not part of the objectives — were the tears. We would barely get into the first question: "How are you?" before the tears would start to come. And before the ninety minutes were over, the tears were on both sides: the ones sharing and we who were listening. Sometimes they were tears of joy: a special event that had been moving and meaningful. Most often they were tears of concern and pain. They felt alone in their struggles and were sure they were the only ones who had them. There were tensions in the congregations and very often we heard the phrase: "We haven't been able to say this to each other till now." There was serious discussion with each other, but seldom negative confrontation. Often they ended up talking more to each other than to us. Our role was to be there and to listen in.

They shared much wisdom, and we made a point of jotting it down. We tried to decipher the common themes and threads that we heard again and again. I promised them a full report of what we had heard. In places where there was disagreement with MC Canada, we would often hear: "We know you may not be able to do what we want, but at least we know that you have heard us, and we will trust your judgment." It was evident that there was pain, struggle, challenge, and life in the congregations. Most of all, there were golden hearts: persons who were doing their best with what they had. One elderly lady with shining and smiling eyes said: "Our congregation is like a little songbird. We have everything we need to be who we are." At a rural church, they reported that the men had gotten tired of the persistent announcements by the women about the "ladies' salad suppers" so they had organized the "men's meat meal." The conversations were meaningful and informative. Only once in 233 visits did I lose my patience with what we heard. And, of course, that one experience also sticks in my mind.

We finished the visits in October 2006. The last congregation was the Mannheim Mennonite Church close to Kitchener, Ontario. Again we were warmly received, and after the conversation they had organized a small celebration. There was cake, and I was given a T-shirt saying: "I survived the God's People Now Tour." There were hugs and smiles all around. I appreciated the thoughtfulness of the congregational leaders.

After the visits were finished, I wrote a full report to our general board. I filtered what we had heard into ten categories and wrote a little book with these ten chapters. It was published with the title *God's People Now: Face to Face with Mennonite Church Canada*. In the appendix, I included about 800 wise sayings that we had sifted from the conversations. Some are funny, some are sad. All are very revealing about the life of the church. This was wisdom from the pews at its best. The book sold almost 1,000 copies in the first month.

Without a doubt, the themes that emerged formed the foundation of my entire time in the office till 2010. I think we had put our finger on the pulse and were able to find small ways of addressing what we heard. The impact of the visits bubbled up all the time, often in unexpected places and ways. I had learned somewhere that leadership is like a bank account. You must have something in the account if later you wish to withdraw from it. I think this is what the visits did for me and for my time as general secretary. The visits filled my bank account with trust, relationships, knowledge, information, and wisdom from the pews. I know there were times later when I had to draw heavily on the account and the level of credits went down. But I always felt there was more in the account that I could count on. I still do to this day. I believe it was the most important leadership initiative I have ever engaged in my life of leadership in the church.

Aging and Grandparenting

I should not really collate aging with grandparenting. The two are very distinct — in some ways. Yet, there is an undeniable connection between the two. Twenty-three years ago, my primary self-identity was not defined by aging. I was thriving, challenged in my work, and healthy to the core. Life was good. If you would have asked about me, very likely the question of age would not have been on my agenda.

But twenty-three years ago is also when our first grandchild was born — a beautiful baby boy. Along with the joy of seeing new life in our tribe, it also served to remind us of the reality of aging. The birth of a grandson signalled that something had happened; but it kind of crept up on us. Our own child had been born, had grown to adulthood, had learned to make his own decisions, had married, developed a career, and was now a father. If all those things had happened to him, it must mean that we, too, had added substantially to our years. I was indeed getting on; I was closing in on the mid-fifties.

It was a good reminder. This first grandson was then followed by five more grandchildren — three boys and three girls altogether. It is a delight to watch our own children become parents. It is even more of a delight to see the little ones grow, develop, mature, and choose their paths.

One of the great things of grandparenting is to see the biblical promise of individuality and giftedness unfolding right before our eyes. It is amazing how different personalities are evident almost from day one. They may have some physical resemblances to each other and to the parents, yet they are entirely unique beings. And as they develop and mature, the giftedness and diversity becomes evident. What a gift to see God's love for diversity underscored in them again and again.

Another good thing about grandparenting is the opportunity to watch our own children develop their parenting skills, generate habits, and creatively implement their own values that have been growing over the years. They come face to face with what is acceptable and what is not. They notice that their children begin to mime their language, attitudes, actions, and priorities. In a sense, they have to define what wagons they will hitch their horses to. Again, the giftedness and diversity of each one shines through. Another gift to behold.

There is a twenty-one-year age gap between our first grandchild and our last one (at least we've been told it's the last one). The gap between the next ones is ten years. These are visible signals of the passing of generations. It is clear that they are not of the same generations — another reminder of our own aging. If a generation or two has passed among them, what does that say about us? They must surely view us ancient relics of times past, even as we tend to think of them as the "next" generation. It focuses our thinking, and we can't help but wonder what their lives will look like. What we thought was novel is normal for them. What we thought was optional or luxury, for them is necessity and obligatory. They may well live into the twenty-second century. What kind of a world lies before them?

We love our grandchildren — each one — and are proud of them — each one. We look for ways to be present in their lives. We are grateful for their parents and admire their parenting skills. Where did they learn to be such creative parents? Certainly not from us. We are impressed by them and wonder where they get their energy from. And we are reminded that we too had that kind of boundless energy. Another vivid connection to aging.

I retired from my work at the age of sixty-five. I resisted taking the step, but it was time, and I knew it. Thankfully, in our culture retirement does not have a fixed definition. We can retire but then define it in ways that suits who we are. We were very fortunate. One of my colleagues at MC Canada figured out a creative way of keeping some of my gifts on the go, but without carrying the administrative responsibilities. She called it a "missional ambassador." The Church invited us to offer our teaching gifts to the global church. These years have been unexpectedly rich, and we are grateful for the initiative that made it possible.

We have been to Vietnam, Indonesia (twice), India (six times), China (three times), Philippines (three times), Hong Kong, Macau, Australia, New Zealand, Europe, Zimbabwe, South Africa (three times), Zambia, Ethiopia, and most countries in Latin America, and Cuba. We have had the privilege of getting to know the Church from the inside in each of these settings. We have interacted with pastors and leaders. We have engaged with them on the challenges they face. We have shared insight and experience with them. We have felt the warm hospitality and experienced their willingness to be vulnerable. It has been stimulating, interesting, and humbling.

It has given us a glimpse of the potential advantages of aging. One congregation in our nationwide church has a group called UBJs: Unencumbered By Jobs. There are advantages to that.

Thus far, aging has been a welcome journey. It has given us opportunities we would not have dreamed of. But we are also getting to the end of that stage. I am aware of another stage coming. Watching others go through that stage has, at times, been difficult. Irene's mother used to say: "The golden years are not very golden." For others this has meant losing partners, sometimes to death, sometimes to dementia and Alzheimer's. It has meant increased vulnerability in health and restricted mobility. For some it has meant fighting the diseases common to aging people. It means stepping back several more steps and letting go of even more. It has meant dislocation and finding more secure places to live. It has meant letting go of elements that have been critical to our identity for decades.

But we have also watched as grace seems to abound, love is extended, and wisdom seems to be more profound. We have seen the focus shifting to the big picture and seen how helpful it is to be reminded again of a broader vision. We have seen patience nurtured. We have seen ways in which the value of little things returns: the songs of the birds, the beauty of the flowers, the taste of tomatoes, the joy of an ice cream cone. These little things are not less profound than the big ones. They have gained strength in the wisdom they teach.

Most of all, we continue to see the faithfulness of God in our lives and in the lives of others. And we are grateful. Life has been good. Life is good. God is good. And we are creatures of God's goodness.

IV

Summary Reflections

In 1992, I developed a serious back pain that Colombian doctors were unable to diagnose. After several weeks of trying, they suggested going back to Canada because they could not pinpoint the problem, and it was getting worse by the day. They didn't say in so many words, but they gave us the impression that it was serious — perhaps a terminal illness. Those weeks gave me a chance to reflect on my life and, to my surprise, I was at peace. Already then, I knew that my life had been beyond blessed; it had been rich, meaningful, and good. As it turned out, they did finally diagnose a bad ulcer, which, with treatment, disappeared and has never come back.

Now, at the age of 75, I again have many opportunities to reflect. My sense of peace has not changed. Now, even more than then, I have experienced life to the fullest. I feel a bit like Abraham in that God promised to bless him, and through his family, bless many other families too. It doesn't get better than that. That promise has again become real, and we are grateful.

At one point quite early in our marriage, Irene and I realized that it was more helpful to think of a five-year plan rather than longer-range plans or no plan at all. Five years seemed to work well. It was enough time to dig in, get immersed, experience, and learn, but not too much time to sink into ruts that we wanted to avoid. It also wasn't too little time that would make our life segments superficial and flitting. At times, this sense of five-year plans was more overt than at other times. Looking back now, I can easily identify at least eight of these segments.

We have lived and worked in five countries and have "adopted" one other with dozens of meaningful assignments, although we have never been able to live there. We have had sixteen homes in nine distinct locations. Each one has provided us with a circle of good friends that we cherish to this day. The drawback has been that our children have not had a permanent sense of "home," at least not geographically. We have worked hard to make each location a "home" but acknowledge that attachment to location is also a significant and meaningful ingredient of identity. This ingredient has been anaemic, and we may have underestimated its importance. We are sorry if that is the case. While there have been many advantages to this model, there surely have also been times when they have experienced this as unstable and challenging in making lifelong friends and putting down roots. They still have difficulty answering the simple question: Where are you from? Each one has both struggled and thrived in his own way, weaving together the advantages with the disadvantages. They, too, have lived a rich but unorthodox life. We are proud of each one. But the verdict must come from them. I suspect that it is never quite final as they continue to experience life as "third culture kids."

My final words must focus on Irene — my wife and partner for fifty-five years and counting. She has been a pillar in our marriage and family. Her persistent capacity to be grace-full, gentle, hospitable, kind, grateful, and loving has definitively shaped every part of our journey together. She has given of herself to me, to our family, and to countless others. She finds important ways of doing what really matters and what makes a big difference in the lives of people. She has demonstrated the gift of administration in the truest sense of the word: persistently transforming lofty ideals and ideas into tangible expressions of meaningful relationships. She is an expert in getting the rubber to hit the road. I am fortunate and grateful for this journey together.

V

Photo Gallery

My siblings (from left to right back row): Peter, Linda, David, Mary, Jim. (front row): Jack, Henry; 1999.

Mom and Dad with three sons (from left to right): Bryan, Andrew, Derek.

Family (from left to right front row): Zoe, Matthew, Eden, Irene, Samantha, James. (second row): Shegofa (our "adopted" granddaughter from Afghanistan), Julie, Derek. (back row): Karen, Simon, Bryan, Jack, Andrew, Rebecca.

Irene's siblings (from left to right): Victor, Irene, Walter, Lorna, John.

Cuban pastors and leaders at workshop, 2020

Jack and Irene at Fraser Lake, Ontario, during family camping, 2013.

Irene's parents: Susie Neufeld and David Penner
on their 25th wedding anniversary, 1967.

Home farmhouse.

VI

Annotated Timeline

Birthday: February 15, 1945:

Born, Robert John Suderman in the Winkler, Manitoba hospital.

Parents: Jacob and Margaret (Epp) Suderman

Farm: Greenfarm School District

Location of farm: From the Winkler, Manitoba corner of Highway #14 and Country Road #32, go one mile north, one mile east. Our farm started on the northeast corner of that intersection and continued east for 1/2 mile, and north for 1 mile.

School:

Kindergarten: May and June, 1951: Greenfarm School District

Grades 1-8: 1951-59: Greenfarm School District

Grade 9: 1959-60: at home

Grades 10-12: 1960-63: Winkler High School

Teacher's college: 1963-1964: called Normal School, Winnipeg. Corner of Grant Ave. and Shaftesbury Blvd. (where the Canadian Mennonite University now is).

BA: 1967: University of Winnipeg

BEd: 1968: University of Manitoba

Masters of Arts in Religion: 1975: Associated Mennonite Biblical Seminaries, Elkhart, Indiana

Doctor of Theology: 1994: Javeriana Pontifical University, Bogotá, Colombia

Baptism:

Winkler Bergthaler Church, June 10, 1962. There were thirty-one young people baptized in the group I was in, including Irene Penner, later to become my wife.

Marriage:

Winkler Bergthaler Church, August 1, 1965.

Married to Irene Francis Penner, born July 25, 1944, also from Winkler.

Children:

Bryan Douglas, born in Winnipeg, Manitoba, January 16, 1969
Weldon Derek, born in Winnipeg, Manitoba, February 4, 1972
Andrew Gregory, born in Rosthern, Saskatchewan, May 11, 1978

Children married:

Bryan married Julie Moyer, June 13, 1992, in Waterloo, Ontario
Derek married Rebecca Seiling, July 3, 1999, in Elora, Ontario
Andrew married Karen Brown, July 5, 2003, in Didsbury, Alberta

Grandchildren:

Matthew Moyer Suderman, born to Bryan Moyer Suderman and Julie Moyer, in Winnipeg, June 6, 1997
Zoe Jeanene Suderman, born to Derek Suderman and Rebecca Seiling, Stouffville, Ontario, December 18, 2003
Eden Suderman, born to Derek Suderman and Rebecca Seiling, Waterloo, Ontario, July 14, 2006
Samantha Joy Suderman, born to Andrew and Karen Suderman, Pietermaritzburg, South Africa, October 17, 2010
James Robert Suderman, born to Andrew and Karen Suderman, Pietermaritzburg, South Africa, July 3, 2013

Simon Joshua Suderman, born to Andrew and Karen Suderman, Harrisonburg, Virginia, August 21, 2018

Employment History:

Teacher: Zion School District, 1964-65: Zion was a country school 3.5 miles west of Winkler on the #3 Highway, and 1/2 mile north.

Teacher: Meath School District, 1965-66: Meath was 4 miles east and 11/2 miles south of Winkler.

Teacher: Westgate Mennonite Collegiate, 1968-1973, Winnipeg, Manitoba.

Bus Driver: Grey Goose Bus Line, 1972-74, Winnipeg, Manitoba: summer employment.

Principal: Rosthern Junior College, 1975-1980, Rosthern, Saskatchewan.

Mission Worker: with the Commission on Overseas Mission, headquarters in Newton, Kansas, 1980-1996. This was divided into the following segments:

1980-81: Language school in San José, Costa Rica (Instituto de Lengua Española);

1981-85: Professor of New Testament and Theology at the Seminario Teológico Bautista in Cochabamba, Bolivia;

1985-89: Doctoral Studies at the Toronto School of Theology, with residency in Kitchener, Ontario;

1989-94: Founding Director of CLARA (Centro Latinioamericano de Recursos Anabautistas), Bogotá, Colombia; and Founding Director and Professor of the Seminario Bíblico Menonita de Colombia, Bogotá, Colombia;

1994-96: Itineration for COM in North America, with residence in Winnipeg, Manitoba.

Executive Secretary, Resources Commission of the Conference of Mennonites in Canada, with headquarters in Winnipeg, Manitoba, 1996-99;

Executive Secretary, Mission Commission of the Conference of Mennonites in Canada, with headquarters in Winnipeg, Manitoba, 1999-2001;

Executive Secretary, Mennonite Church Canada Witness, with headquarters in Winnipeg, Manitoba, 2001-2005;

General Secretary of Mennonite Church Canada, with headquarters in Winnipeg, Manitoba, 2005-10;

Retirement: July 2010;

Secretary of the Peace Commission of Mennonite World Conference, 2012-15;

Missional Ambassador for Mennonite Church Canada, 2010-16;

Learning Tour Leader, with TourMagination out of Waterloo, Ontario: tours to Cuba, Paraguay, Colombia, 2015-2020.

Move to New Hamburg, Ontario: July 31, 2011, 15 Rollingbrook Lane, New Hamburg.

VII

Other Books Published

The Replacement Pattern in the Fourth Gospel: A Persecuted Community Confronts its Past. Robert J. Suderman: Bogotá, Colombia: La Pontificia Universidad Javeriana, 1994.

Discipulado Cristiano al Servicio del Reino. Roberto J. Suderman: Ciudad de Guatemala, Guatemala: Ediciones Semilla/CLARA, 1994.

Tengan Valor: Yo he Vencido al Mundo. Roberto J. Suderman: Ciudad de Guatemala, Guatemala: Ediciones Semilla/CLARA, 1998.

Calloused Hands, Courageous Souls. Robert J. Suderman: translated by W. Derek Suderman: Monrovia, California: MARC, 1998.

God's People Now! Face to Face with Mennonite Church Canada. Robert J. Suderman: Waterloo, Ontario: Herald Press, 2007.

Re-Imagining the Church: Implications of Being a People in the World. Robert J. Suderman: edited by Andrew G. Suderman: Eugene, Oregon: Wipf and Stock, 2016.

About the Author

Robert J. Suderman provides glimpses into his life journey from a farmboy on a small farm in Manitoba, to retirement from his role as General Secretary of Mennonite Church Canada. He has served the church in various capacities for fifty-two years as teacher, administrator, writer, and leader. Suderman, with Irene, his wife of fifty-five years, now enjoys retirement in New Hamburg, Ontario. He is an active member of First Mennonite Church in Kitchener, Ontario, and continues to be work in various informal, volunteer consulting capacities with church-related organizations. He is, perhaps, best known for his persistent passion for the critical — non-optional — role of the church in understanding God's reconciling mission to the world.

Robert and Irene have three sons, three daughters-in-law, and six grandchildren — all of whom bring joy, blessing, and love into their life.

CPSIA information can be obtained
at www.ICGtesting.com
Printed in the USA
BVHW070558190920
589088BV00002B/11

9 780228 833512